The Christmas Message

Queen Elizabeth II
Describes the Significance of Christmas

Edited by
Geoffrey Waugh

The Christmas Message

Queen Elizabeth II
Describes the Significance of Christmas
2018

Originally available as *The Christmas Message: Reflections on the Significance of Christmas from The Queen's Christmas Broadcasts.*

Cover photo: Her Majesty Queen Elizabeth II, in the first colour television broadcast of her Christmas Message, 1967. This book commemorates the 50th Anniversary of that broadcast, and also commemorates the 60th Anniversary of The Queen's first television broadcast in 1957, and 65 years of annual Christmas Messages from 1952.

Basic Edition: ISBN 978-1719592536 (in print)
Basic Edition eBook: ASIN B07DB4HVNC
Gift Edition: ISBN 978-1719592543 (in colour)
Gift Edition eBook: ASIN B07DB5PHVG
Available at Amazon, Kindle and Distributors
Printed in Great Britain, Europe and America

Renewal Journal Publications
www.renewaljournal.com
Brisbane, Australia

Renewal Journal

Logo: scribe's lamp & parchment
and servant's basin & towel
in the light of the cross

♛

A tribute to

the Christmas Broadcasts of

Her Majesty

Queen Elizabeth II

with appreciation

Endorsements

1. I haven't seen anyone else draw the events of the last 65 years together in this way before. Using the Queen's speeches not only ties in the unfolding events of our time but reveals a deep spiritual glue that provides a fascinating and intimate insight into the personal life of our Queen. A fascinating read. 5 Stars. - Rev Philip Waugh (Minister)

2. 'The Christmas Message' is an appealing, highly unusual and very creative anthology. After an introduction about the Queen's public expression of faith, Geoff Waugh provides a selection of noteworthy passages about Christmas from the Queen's Christmas messages from 1952 to 2017. He sets them into context by brief historical references, photos, and Christmas stamps. Finally there is an epilogue of famous Christmas hymns and carols including those used in the Christmas Broadcasts. This book would be the perfect Christmas present. - Alison Sherrington (Author)

3. The strength of the Commonwealth of Nations is the application of Christ's teaching of peace and goodwill to all, a thread that follows through each of the broadcasts of Her Majesty's Christmas Messages and is embodied in The Queen's own testament in these messages. The core of the book is the excerpts from The Queen's messages. Geoff introduces each broadcast with a short commentary on the events of that year and highlights The Queen's words in the context of each year, accompanied with appropriate photographs and commemorative stamps.

The birth of Christ, now widely celebrated as Christmas throughout the world, is the background and basis for The Queen's speeches. A comprehensive appendix lists resources used in many broadcasts together with words of the more common carols. The appendix is a fitting conclusion to this new and innovative approach to the Christmas Story and its clear message of peace and goodwill to all. It is a rewarding experience to read it from cover to cover. - Don Hill (Consultant)

Contents

Introduction

The Christmas Message, first told and written 2000 years ago, is now celebrated around the world. Christmas Day is a public holiday in many countries. Families gather to celebrate, share gifts, look back on the past year and look forward to another year.

Millions of people attend churches at Christmas to hear and sing the Christmas Message. Popular readings at Christmas from the ancient stories about the unique baby's birth were first written on parchment in the Gospels of Luke and Matthew. Luke tells the story this way, as read for over 400 years in the classical Authorized Version, known as the King James Version of 1611:

> And it came to pass in those days, that there went out a decree from Caesar Augustus that all the world should be taxed.
>
> 2 (And this taxing was first made when Cyrenius was governor of Syria.)
>
> 3 And all went to be taxed, every one into his own city.
>
> 4 And Joseph also went up from Galilee, out of the city of Nazareth, into Judaea, unto the city of David, which is called Bethlehem; (because he was of the house and lineage of David:)
>
> 5 To be taxed with Mary his espoused wife, being great with child.
>
> 6 And so it was, that, while they were there, the days were accomplished that she should be delivered.
>
> 7 And she brought forth her firstborn son, and wrapped him in swaddling clothes, and laid him in a manger; because there was no room for them in the inn.
>
> 8 And there were in the same country shepherds abiding in the field, keeping watch over their flock by night.
>
> 9 And, lo, the angel of the Lord came upon them, and the glory of the Lord shone round about them: and they were sore afraid.
>
> 10 And the angel said unto them, Fear not: for, behold, I bring you good tidings of great joy, which shall be to all people.
>
> 11 For unto you is born this day in the city of David a Saviour, which is Christ the Lord.
>
> 12 And this shall be a sign unto you; Ye shall find the babe wrapped in swaddling clothes, lying in a manger.
>
> 13 And suddenly there was with the angel a multitude of the heavenly host praising God, and saying,
>
> 14 Glory to God in the highest, and on earth peace, good will toward men. (Luke 2:1-14 KJV)

Matthew continues the story this way:

Now when Jesus was born in Bethlehem of Judaea in the days of Herod the king, behold, there came wise men from the east to Jerusalem,

2 Saying, Where is he that is born King of the Jews? for we have seen his star in the east, and are come to worship him.

3 When Herod the king had heard these things, he was troubled, and all Jerusalem with him.

4 And when he had gathered all the chief priests and scribes of the people together, he demanded of them where Christ should be born.

5 And they said unto him, In Bethlehem of Judaea: for thus it is written by the prophet,

6 And thou Bethlehem, in the land of Juda, art not the least among the princes of Juda: for out of thee shall come a Governor, that shall rule my people Israel.

7 Then Herod, when he had privily called the wise men, enquired of them diligently what time the star appeared.

8 And he sent them to Bethlehem, and said, Go and search diligently for the young child; and when ye have found him, bring me word again, that I may come and worship him also.

9 When they had heard the king, they departed; and, lo, the star, which they saw in the east, went before them, till it came and stood over where the young child was.

10 When they saw the star, they rejoiced with exceeding great joy.

11 And when they were come into the house, they saw the young child with Mary his mother, and fell down, and worshipped him: and when they had opened their treasures, they presented unto him gifts; gold, and frankincense and myrrh.

12 And being warned of God in a dream that they should not return to Herod, they departed into their own country another way.

13 And when they were departed, behold, the angel of the Lord appeareth to Joseph in a dream, saying, Arise, and take the young child and his mother, and flee into Egypt, and be thou there until I bring thee word: for Herod will seek the young child to destroy him.

14 When he arose, he took the young child and his mother by night, and departed into Egypt:

15 And was there until the death of Herod: that it might be fulfilled which was spoken of the Lord by the prophet, saying, Out of Egypt have I called my son.

(Matthew 2:1-15 KJV)

The translators of the New Revised Standard Version of the Bible, first published in 1989, acknowledged the majesty of the King James Version this way in their introductory word "to the reader":

> In the course of time the King James Version came to be regarded as "the Authorized Version." With good reason it has been termed "the noblest monument of English prose," and it has entered, as no other book has, into the making of the personal character of the public institutions of the English-speaking peoples. We owe to it an incalculable debt.

Many people now prefer the New King James Version (NKJV). Those who prefer more current or modern language may like to meditate on the translation of these timeless stories in the New Revised Standard Version (NRSV), now read in many churches and used for personal study and enjoyment. The NRSV uses inclusive language (as does the original Hebrew and Greek) and includes useful section headings. Where the passage under a section heading is repeated, or has a similar passage elsewhere in the Bible, the NRSV heading gives the other references. Headings for unique passages, not repeated elsewhere, have no references, as in these unique Christmas stories in Luke and Matthew.

The Birth of Jesus

In those days a decree went out from Emperor Augustus that all the world should be registered. 2 This was the first registration and was taken while Quirinius was governor of Syria. 3 All went to their own towns to be registered. 4 Joseph also went from the town of Nazareth in Galilee to Judea, to the city of David called Bethlehem, because he was descended from the house and family of David. 5 He went to be registered with Mary, to whom he was engaged and who was expecting a child. 6 While they were there, the time came for her to deliver her child. 7 And she gave birth to her firstborn son and wrapped him in bands of cloth, and laid him in a manger, because there was no place for them in the inn.

The Shepherds and the Angels

8 In that region there were shepherds living in the fields, keeping watch over their flock by night. 9 Then an angel of the Lord stood before them, and the glory of the Lord shone around them, and they were terrified. 10 But the angel said to them, 'Do not be afraid; for see—I am bringing you good news of great joy for all the people: 11 to you is born this day in the city of David a Saviour, who is the Messiah, the Lord. 12 This will be a sign for you: you will find a child wrapped in bands of cloth and lying in a manger.' 13 And suddenly there was with the angel a multitude of the heavenly host, praising God and saying,

14 'Glory to God in the highest heaven,
   and on earth peace among those whom he favours!'

(Luke 2:1-14 NRSV)

The Visit of the Wise Men

In the time of King Herod, after Jesus was born in Bethlehem of Judea, wise men from the East came to Jerusalem, 2 asking, 'Where is the child who has been born king of the Jews? For we observed his star at its rising, and have come to pay him homage.' 3 When King Herod heard this, he was frightened, and all Jerusalem with him; 4 and calling together all the chief priests and scribes of the people, he inquired of them where the Messiah was to be born. 5 They told him, 'In Bethlehem of Judea; for so it has been written by the prophet:

6 "And you, Bethlehem, in the land of Judah,
    are by no means least among the rulers of Judah;
for from you shall come a ruler
    who is to shepherd my people Israel."'

7 Then Herod secretly called for the wise men and learned from them the exact time when the star had appeared. 8 Then he sent them to Bethlehem, saying, 'Go and search diligently for the child; and when you have found him, bring me word so that I may also go and pay him homage.' 9 When they had heard the king, they set out; and there, ahead of them, went the star that they had seen at its rising, until it stopped over the place where the child was. 10 When they saw that the star had stopped, they were overwhelmed with joy. 11 On entering the house, they saw the child with Mary his mother; and they knelt down and paid him homage. Then, opening their treasure-chests, they offered him gifts of gold, frankincense, and myrrh. 12 And having been warned in a dream not to return to Herod, they left for their own country by another road.

The Escape to Egypt

13 Now after they had left, an angel of the Lord appeared to Joseph in a dream and said, 'Get up, take the child and his mother, and flee to Egypt, and remain there until I tell you; for Herod is about to search for the child, to destroy him.' 14 Then Joseph got up, took the child and his mother by night, and went to Egypt, 15 and remained there until the death of Herod. This was to fulfil what had been spoken by the Lord through the prophet, 'Out of Egypt I have called my son.'

(Matthew 2:1-15 NRSV)

These Christmas stories are Gospel readings used in church lectionaries in the Advent and Christmas seasons in December each year. Christmas Day is a time when millions of people enjoy celebrating Christmas in church services where these and similar readings are used. It is also a time when millions enjoy singing Christmas Carols, such as those included in the Appendix of this book, in Carols by Candlelight and at other concerts. Many Carols tell these Christmas stories in beautiful, poetic lyrics.

Another valued Christmas tradition for millions of us has been listening to the Royal Christmas Message which is broadcast around the world on Christmas Day.

The Queen's first Christmas Message (1952), broadcast to millions of listeners, reminded us that "Peace on earth, Goodwill toward men" is the eternal message of Christmas, and the desire of us all. The Queen's Christmas Broadcasts give us her compassionate review of the year and describe the significance of Christmas, the celebration of the baby born king, the King of kings and Lord of lords.

The formal name of her Christmas Broadcast is 'Her Majesty's Most Gracious Speech.'

King George V, The Queen's grandfather, gave the first Royal Christmas Message in 1932. King George VI commenced the custom of an annual Royal Christmas Message in 1939 at the outbreak of the Second World War (1939-1945), just 21 years after the end of the First World War (1914-1918). King George VI ended his first Christmas broadcast with encouragement from the poem by **Minnie Louise Haskins** titled *God Knows*:

> *I said to the man who stood at the Gate of the Year, "Give me a light that I may tread safely into the unknown." And he replied, "Go out into the darkness, and put your hand into the Hand of God. That shall be to you better than light, and safer than a known way."*

The poem continues:

So I went forth, and finding the Hand of God, trod gladly into the night.
And He led me towards the hills and the breaking of day in the lone East.

So heart be still:
What need our little life
Our human life to know,
If God hath comprehension?
In all the dizzy strife
Of things both high and low,
God hideth His intention.

God knows. His will
Is best. The stretch of years
Which wind ahead, so dim
To our imperfect vision,
Are clear to God. Our fears
Are premature; In Him,
All time hath full provision.

Then rest: until
God moves to lift the veil
From our impatient eyes,
When, as the sweeter features
Of Life's stern face we hail,
Fair beyond all surmise
God's thought around His creatures
Our mind shall fill.[1]

---

[1] *God Knows,* privately published by the author in the collection, *The Desert,* 1912.

The King's quotation of "The Gate of the Year" brought it to public attention and it became an inspiration to millions throughout the world. Widely reproduced and quoted, including on the following Sunday, New Year's Eve, December 31, 1939, the poem has continued to comfort and inspire many generations.

The book *The Servant Queen and the King She Serves,* published for Queen Elizabeth II's 90th birthday, with a Foreword by the Queen, says that the young Princess Elizabeth, aged 13, handed the poem to her father. Queen Elizabeth The Queen Mother had its words engraved on plaques on the gates of the King George VI Memorial Chapel at Windsor Castle, where the King was interred in 1952, as she was in 2002, having lived to 101.

The annual Queen's Christmas Broadcasts continue to inspire a worldwide audience. For millions, as for our family, it has been an eagerly anticipated part of Christmas Day, often following celebrations including the joyful carols of the morning church service, sharing family gifts, and enjoying the Christmas family lunch or dinner together. Our family, in Australia's summer, would sprawl around the floor and lounge chairs to relax and listen to the broadcast of the Royal Christmas Message on radio and, later on, on television. This was a welcome break amid the family's festive games such as trying out new toys or sports gear. The next day, on the Boxing Day holiday, we were back watching English and Australian cricketers compete in The Ashes series.

As technology developed, The Queen's Christmas Broadcast came to us with increasing and impressive sophistication. The early years of the crackling wireless from 1952 gave way to the magic of sight with black and white television from 1957, then to the splendours of colour TV from 1967. From 1959 the pre-recorded broadcasts gave increasing opportunity for relevant film footage to be interspersed with The Queen speaking. Millions appreciate her compassionate observations about events of the past year and about the significance of Christmas.

Jon Kuhrt wrote a blog about The Queen's Christmas messages. While he worked with people affected by homelessness, offending and addictions at the West London Mission he was impressed by comments in the 2014 broadcast. Jon wrote: "I have not been a committed viewer (apart from when I am at my Mum's when it is compulsory viewing). So I went back and read her previous Christmas messages over the last 5 years."

Here, I have adapted Jon's Resistance and Renewal blog in which he describes how The Queen's Christmas messages are a model of how to talk about faith in the public sphere. (https://resustanceandrenewal.net/2014/12/28/the-queens-christmas-message-a-model-of-how-to-talk-about-faith-in-the-public-sphere).

1) The Queen speaks personally
"It is my prayer this Christmas Day that Jesus' example and teaching will continue to bring people together to give the best of themselves in the service of others." (2012)
"For me, the life of Jesus Christ, the prince of peace, whose birth we celebrate today, is an inspiration and an anchor in my life." (2014)
Personal testimony is significant and convincing, causing respect in those listening. The Queen is *personal* in the way she speaks, using words like 'for me'; 'my life' and 'my prayer'.

2) The Queens speaks compassionately

"Despite being displaced and persecuted throughout his short life, Christ's unchanging message was not one of revenge or violence but simply that we should love one another." (2015)

"Christ's example helps me see the value of doing small things with great love, whoever does them and whatever they themselves believe." (2016)

Consistently, The Queen and the Royal Family show deep concern for the bereaved and suffering, both in personal contact and in correspondence. The heart of Christmas is about God's love for everyone, especially the hurting and fallen.

3) The Queen speaks inclusively

"The Christmas message shows us that this love is for everyone. There is no one beyond its reach." (2013)

"Christ's example has taught me to seek to respect and value all people, of whatever faith or none." (2014)

God's love is for *all people* and believing in this love leads us to respect and value everyone. Jon adds, "It resonated with my own experience of meeting The Queen in 1997, when she came to open a new hostel for young homeless people that I was managing. I showed her round and introduced her to all the residents. I had expected it to be quite formal and awkward but I remember how adept she was at talking to such a diverse range of people."

4) The Queen speaks about Jesus

"This is the time of year when we remember that God sent his only son 'to serve, not to be served'. He restored love and service to the centre of our lives in the person of Jesus Christ." (2012)

"God sent into the world a unique person – neither a philosopher nor a general ... but a Saviour, with the power to forgive." (2011)

The Queen talks directly about the person at the heart of Christmas, the reason for celebrating. That includes both the example and achievement of Jesus and makes orthodox theology accessible to the widest possible audience.

5) The Queen speaks about faith in action

"Forgiveness lies at the heart of the Christian faith. It can heal broken families, it can restore friendships and it can reconcile divided communities. It is in forgiveness that we feel the power of God's love." (2011)

"For Christians, as for all people of faith, reflection, meditation and prayer help us to renew ourselves in God's love, as we strive daily to become better people." (2013)

Reconciliation, service and love flow from Christian commitment. The Queen talks about what faith *does*. It makes a difference to how we live and helps us to be 'better people'.

The following pages give brief quotations about the significance and meaning of Christmas drawn from The Queen's Christmas Broadcasts, 1952-2017, commemorating the baby born King – the King of kings and Lord of lords.

The Christmas Message

Queen Elizabeth II describes the Significance of Christmas

"Peace on earth, Goodwill toward men" ~
the eternal message of Christmas, and the desire of us all
(The Queen's First Christmas Broadcast, 1952)

The Queen has spoken about the significance of Christmas to more people than anyone else in history

1952

Queen Elizabeth II has been Queen of the United Kingdom, Australia, Canada, and New Zealand since 6 February 1952. She is Queen of 12 countries that became independent since 1952, and is Head of the Commonwealth of Nations, a free association of independent member nations (commonly known as *the Commonwealth*), comprising over 50 sovereign states. The Queen carries the blessings and responsibilities of her reign with grace and dignity. She understands the value of influence, symbols, tradition and innovation.

Elizabeth II (born 21 April 1926) began her reign at the age of 25 when her father King George VI died. The Queen heard of her Accession while visiting Kenya.

Her first Christmas message, broadcast from the same desk and chair used by her father and grandfather, continued the tradition of Christmas Broadcasts passed on to her by George V and George VI. The Queen thanked her people for their loyalty and affection in the first months of her reign. She referred to the British Commonwealth and Empire as an *"immense union of nations"* that was like a family and which *"can be a great power for good – a force which I believe can be of immeasurable benefit to all humanity."*

The Queen spoke about her forthcoming Coronation where she would dedicate herself anew to serve her people, concluding:

I want to ask you all, whatever your religion may be, to pray for me on that day - to pray that God may give me wisdom and strength to carry out the solemn promises I shall be making, and that I may faithfully serve Him and you, all the days of my life. May God bless and guide you all through the coming year.

This message, and the broadcasts until 1956, were simulcast on television in sound without visuals. From 1957, millions of people have seen and heard The Queen on television and on radio on Christmas Day.

Unlike her other speeches prepared for her by officials, Her Majesty writes her own Christmas messages, assisted by her husband and her aides.

Quotations about the significance of Christmas from The Queen's Christmas Broadcasts are reproduced in this book in **bold italics,** as on the following right-hand pages, often reminding us, as in this first Christmas Broadcast, that *"Peace on earth, Goodwill toward men" is the eternal message of Christmas, and the desire of us all.*

The Queen's first Christmas Broadcast

Each Christmas, at this time, my beloved father broadcast a message to his people in all parts of the world. Today I am doing this to you, who are now my people.

As he used to do, I am speaking to you from my own home, where I am spending Christmas with my family; and let me say at once how I hope that your children are enjoying themselves as much as mine are on a day which is especially the children's festival, kept in honour of the Child born at Bethlehem nearly two thousand years ago. ...

Above all, we must keep alive that courageous spirit of adventure that is the finest quality of youth; and by youth I do not just mean those who are young in years; I mean too all those who are young in heart, no matter how old they may be. That spirit still flourishes in this old country and in all the younger countries of our Commonwealth.

On this broad foundation let us set out to build a truer knowledge of ourselves and our fellowmen, to work for tolerance and understanding among the nations and to use the tremendous forces of science and learning for the betterment of man's lot upon this earth. If we can do these three things with courage, with generosity and with humility, then surely we shall achieve that "Peace on earth, Goodwill toward men" which is the eternal message of Christmas, and the desire of us all.

1953

Queen Elizabeth II was crowned monarch of the United Kingdom, Canada, Australia, New Zealand, South Africa, Pakistan and Ceylon on 2 June 1953 at Westminster Abbey, the first coronation to be televised. Among her many titles she is, by the grace of God, Queen, Head of State, Head of the Commonwealth, Defender of the Faith and Supreme Governor of the Church of England. Her Christmas Broadcasts express that Faith.

In 1953 her Royal Christmas Message was broadcast live from **Auckland in New Zealand**, during The Queen and The Duke **of Edinburgh**'s six month tour of the Commonwealth.

That Commonwealth tour included flying to Bermuda and Jamacia in November, then sailing in SS *Gothic* through Panama on a state visit, and to Fiji and Tonga in December and to New Zealand in December and January.

The young Queen talked about her trip and what she hoped to learn and accomplish from the tour. Referring to the Crown as a "personal and loving bond" between herself and her people, she described the Commonwealth as a "world-wide fellowship of nations." She spoke of feeling at home in New Zealand and expressed sympathy to those affected by the **Tangiwai train disaster** the previous night.

This Christmas Broadcast reminded us that **we are celebrating the birth of the Prince of Peace.**

Australian commemorative stamps, 2 June, 1953

Australian commemorative stamps, 2 June 2003

The Queen observed that *the Commonwealth bears no resemblance to the Empires of the past. It is an entirely new conception, built on the highest qualities of the spirit of man: friendship, loyalty and the desire for freedom and peace.*

To that new conception of an equal partnership of nations and races I shall give myself heart and soul every day of my life.

I wished to speak of it from New Zealand this Christmas Day because we are celebrating the birth of the Prince of Peace, who preached the brotherhood of man.

May that brotherhood be furthered by all our thoughts and deeds from year to year. In pursuit of that supreme ideal the Commonwealth is moving steadily towards greater harmony between its many creeds, colours and races despite the imperfections by which, like every human institution, it is beset.

Already, indeed, in the last half-century it has proved itself the most effective and progressive association of peoples which history has yet seen; and its ideal of brotherhood embraces the whole world. To all my peoples throughout the Commonwealth I commend that Christmas hope and prayer.

1954

The Queen broadcast this message from **Sandringham House** at the end of a year in which she, with her husband **The Duke of Edinburgh**, had travelled around the world, **the first British monarch to circumnavigate the globe. The Royal Tour was the biggest single event ever organised in Australia with an estimated 75% of the population coming out to see their monarch.**

The royal tour continued from New Zealand to Australia in February and March, Cocus Islands, Ceylon, Aden, and Uganda in April, and Malta and Gibraltar, with a state visit to Libya in May, returning to London on 15 May. Their two children, Charles and Anne, joined The Queen and her husband in Malta from where they all sailed on the newly commissioned HMY *Britannia*, the royal yacht which became their welcome home away from home until its tearful decommissioning in December 1997.

With the eyes of the world upon her in the media's ceaseless glare, the young Queen learned to smile till her cheeks hurt, shake hands till her arms ached, talk engagingly with strangers, maintain warm eye contact, and only fully relax when in private with her husband. The media sometimes mistook her relaxed or thoughtful expression when she is not smiling as being cross.

The British Empire and Commonwealth Games, formerly the British Empire Games from 1930, were held in Vancouver, Canada from 30 July to 7 August. **The 'Miracle Mile' saw both the gold medallist, Roger Bannister of England, and silver medallist, John Landy of Australia, run sub-four minute races, an** event televised live across the world for the first time. The Duke of Edinburgh officially closed those 5th British Empire and Commonwealth Games where 24 nations participated.

This year's Royal Christmas Message looked appreciatively back on time spent among the Commonwealth people around the globe, including the previous Christmas in the hot sunshine of Auckland in New Zealand.

Acknowledging that we rightly praise the heroes whose courage shines brightly in crisis moments, The Queen also praised the ranks of unknown, unnamed men and women whose work and loyalty contribute so significantly to human progress.

This speech concluded with reference to the humble origins of the Family from whom Light illuminated the world.

Australian Royal Visit commemorative stamps 1954

I have referred to Christmas as the Children's Festival. But this lovely day is not only a time for family reunions, for paper decorations, for roast turkey and plum pudding.

It has, before all, its origin in the homage we pay to a very special Family, who lived long ago in a very ordinary home, in a very unimportant village in the uplands of a small Roman province.

Life in such a place might have been uneventful. But the Light, kindled in Bethlehem and then streaming from the cottage window in Nazareth, has illumined the world for two thousand years. It is in the glow of that bright beam that I wish you all a blessed Christmas and a happy New Year.

1955

Broadcast live from her study at **Sandringham House**, The Queen spoke about opportunities arising from membership of the Commonwealth of Nations.

With the launch of **Independent TV** in the United Kingdom, the sound-only television broadcast was simulcast on both ITV and the BBC Television Service from this year.

Four Castle series postage stamps were issued depicting a castle from each of the countries in the United Kingdom: "Carrickfergus Castle" of Ireland in brown, "Caernarfon Castle" of Wales in red, "Edinburgh Castle" of Scotland in blue, and "Windsor Castle" of England in black.

There was a state visit to Norway in June. The Queen appreciated her visits to the people of many places in England which she had not seen previously and anticipated visiting Nigeria early in the new year, a Commonwealth Nation of thirty million people.

Quoting **John Masefield,** Poet Laureate from his appointment by George V in 1930 to his death in 1967, Elizabeth II included these stirring lines from *The Wanderer* in her speech:

> *Though you have conquered Earth and charted Sea*
> *And planned the courses of all Stars that be,*
> *Adventure on, more wonders are in Thee.*
>
> *Adventure on, for from the littlest clue*
> *Has come whatever worth man ever knew;*
> *The next to lighten all men may be you.*

This Christmas Speech emphasised the indivisible message that there can be no "Peace on earth" without "Goodwill toward men".

Royal Mail Castle Stamps, 1955

The Christmas message to each of us is indivisible; there can be no "Peace on earth" without "Goodwill toward men". Scientists talk of 'chain reaction' - of power releasing yet more power. This principle must be most true when it is applied to the greatest power of all: the power of love.

My beloved grandfather, King George V, in one of his broadcasts when I was a little girl, called upon all his peoples in these words: "Let each of you be ready and proud to give to his country the service of his work, his mind and his heart." That is surely the first step to set in motion the 'chain reaction' of the Powers of Light, to illuminate the new age ahead of us.

And the second step is this: to understand with sympathy the point of view of others, within our own countries and in the Commonwealth, as well as those outside it.

In this way we can bring our unlimited spiritual resources to bear upon the world. As this Christmas passes by, and time resumes its march, let us resolve that the spirit of Christmas shall stay with us as we journey into the unknown year that lies ahead.

1956

The Duke of Edinburgh spoke from HMY *Britannia* during a voyage around the Commonwealth just before The Queen made her speech live from Sandringham House. She referred to The Duke's message which gave her and her children the greatest joy and wished him a good journey before expressing her sadness at being separated from him.

The year had begun with a Royal tour of Nigeria by The Queen and The Duke of Edinburgh, in January-February. They had a state visit to Sweden in June. The year closed with The Duke of Edinburgh touring Commonwealth countries. He opened the Melbourne Olympics in Australia in November 1956 as the royal representative.

The Queen expressed sympathy to those who do not enjoy a united family or cannot be at home for Christmas, or are alone, or have been driven from home as refugees.

Again she compared the Commonwealth to a family in which, despite its differences, *"for the sake of ultimate harmony, the healing power of tolerance, comradeship and love must be allowed to play its part."*

This year's royal message noted that at Christmas *"words and thoughts, taking their inspiration from the birth of the child in Bethlehem long ago, have been carried between us."*

Literary Stamp, A A Milne (1882-1956)

Royal Visit to Nigeria

Once again messages of Christmas greeting have been exchanged around the world.

From all parts of the Commonwealth, and from the remote and lonely spaces of Antarctica, words and thoughts, taking their inspiration from the birth of the child in Bethlehem long ago, have been carried between us upon the invisible wings of twentieth-century science.

Neither the long and troubled centuries that have passed since that child was born, nor the complex scientific developments of our age, have done anything to dim the simple joy and bright hope we all feel when we celebrate his birthday. ...

Particularly on this day of the family festival let us remember those who - like the Holy Family before them - have been driven from their homes by war or violence. We call them 'refugees': let us give them a true refuge: let us see that for them and their children there is room at the Inn. ...

The Queen said that *the healing power of tolerance, comradeship and love must be allowed to play its part. ...*

That each one of us should give this power a chance to do its work is my heartfelt message to you all upon this Christmas Day. I can think of no better resolve to make, nor any better day on which to make it. Let us remember this during our festivities, for it is part of the Christmas message - "Goodwill toward men".

I wish you all a Happy Christmas and a Happy New Year.

1957

This year's Christmas message, read from the Long Library at Sandringham House, was the first one televised. During her speech The Queen read lines from a sheet of paper inserted into John Bunyan's book, *Pilgrim's Progress*. While preparing for the broadcast, she noticed that the wrong book was used so immediately had the right book brought from the library. The bowl of holly on the desk hid the microphone and her dress by her favourite couturier had to fit well with the furnishings, even in black and white. Always supportive, her husband Prince Philip, The Duke of Edinburgh, made a joke to help her relax before she began.

The Queen noted how technology allowed her to be viewed in homes. She hoped that the new medium of television would make her broadcast more personal and direct. Millions gathered around their TV sets in homes, pubs, clubs and shop windows to watch. It was the most watched television since her coronation.

She recalled with appreciation her opening of the new Canadian Parliament in Canada in October, the first Sovereign to do so. The warm welcome of people in her visits with her husband on state visits to **Portugal, France, Denmark and the United States of America and Canada touched her deeply.**

Sunspots caused freak radio conditions resulting in American police radio transmissions interfering with British radio broadcasts. During The Queen's speech some listeners heard an American police officer say "Joe, I'm gonna grab a quick coffee." Many people may have repeated those words straight after this broadcast, adapted to a cup of tea!

This Speech emphasised ageless ideals and values including the importance of religion, morality, honesty, self-restraint and the **courage to** *"stand up for everything that we know is right, everything that is true and honest."*

First annual Australian Christmas stamp

The First Royal Christmas Message televised

Twenty-five years ago my grandfather broadcast the first of these Christmas messages. Today is another landmark because television has made it possible for many of you to see me in your homes on Christmas Day. ...

I very much hope that this new medium will make my Christmas message more personal and direct.

I believe in our qualities and in our strength, I believe that together we can set an example to the world which will encourage upright people everywhere.

I would like to read you a few lines from 'Pilgrim's Progress', because I am sure we can say with Mr Valiant for Truth, these words:

"Though with great difficulty I am got hither, yet now I do not repent me of all the trouble I have been at to arrive where I am. My sword I give to him that shall succeed me in my pilgrimage and my courage and skill to him that can get it. My marks and scars I carry with me, to be a witness for me that I have fought his battles who now will be my rewarder."

I hope that 1958 may bring you God's blessing and all the things you long for.

And so I wish you all, young and old, wherever you may be, all the fun and enjoyment, and the peace of a very happy Christmas.

1958

This final Christmas Message delivered live was broadcast from the Long Library at Sandringham House. It focused on the importance of spiritual and family values. The Speech described some of the journeys soon to be made around the Commonwealth by The Queen and members of the Royal Family.

The Queen responded to requests that her children be shown in the broadcast by saying that she and her husband decided against it as they want their children to grow up as naturally as possible.

There was a state visit to the Netherlands in March

The British Empire and Commonwealth Games, held in Cardiff, Wales, in July with 35 commonwealth nations participating, introduced The Queen's Baton Relay, carried from her at Buckingham Palace in relays to the opening ceremony, a prelude to every Commonwealth Games ever since. The Duke of Edinburgh opened the Games and The Queen declared the Games closed.

This live Broadcast reminded viewers that *"Christmas is just the time to be grateful to those who add fullness to our lives."*

Royal Mail commemorative stamps
6th British Empire and Commonwealth Games

Christmas stamps 1958

To Christians all over the world, Christmas is an occasion for family gatherings and celebrations, for presents and parties, for friendship and good will.

To many of my people Christmas doesn't have the same religious significance, but friendship and good will are common to us all. So it's a good time to remember those around us who are far from home, feeling perhaps strange and lonely. ...

I am sure that many of you have thought about these things before, but it seems to me that Christmas is just the time to be grateful to those who add fullness to our lives.

Even so we need something more. We all need the kind of security that one gets from a happy and united family. Before I return to mine let me once again wish every one of you a very happy Christmas from all of us here at Sandringham, and may God's blessing be with you in the coming year.

1959

The Queen pre-recorded her Christmas Broadcast for the first time, being pregnant with Prince Andrew, who was born the following February, the first child born to a reigning monarch in over a century. The Speech was filmed in Buckingham Palace a week prior to the broadcast.

It conveyed The Queen's best wishes and her gratitude for the warm wishes she had received. The pre-recorded message could to be shipped abroad in advance and broadcast in Australia and New Zealand and other countries on Christmas Day for the first time. The success of the recording ensured that all subsequent Christmas messages have also been pre-recorded. This allowed creative use of other footage and the Sovereign could now enjoy Christmas with her family without the added strain of a live broadcast.

The royal couple visited Canada again in June and July to open St. Lawrence Seaway and to visit other parts of the country as well.

In this Christmas Speech the Queen encouraged listeners to *"celebrate Christmas with thanksgiving and carry its message of peace and good will into the year ahead."*

St Lawrence Seaway commemorative stamp

Christmas stamp 1959

I do not want Christmas to pass by without sending my best wishes for a happy day to all of you who may be listening, and especially to my own peoples in the Commonwealth. ...

As the old year passes, let us celebrate Christmas with thanksgiving and carry its message of peace and good will into the year ahead.

All of us at Sandringham wish you a very happy Christmas.

May God bless you all.

1960

The Queen spoke from **Buckingham Palace** and described an eventful year which included the birth on 19 February of Prince Andrew, The Duke of York, the title given to the sovereign's second son since the 15th century. Princess Margaret, The Queen's sister, married Anthony Armstrong-Jones at Westminster Abbey on 6 May.

Nigeria gained independence while remaining part of the Commonwealth.

Disasters to which The Queen referred included that year's earthquake in Morocco where 12,000 died, the deaths of 69 protesters in Sharpeville, South Africa, and an explosion killing 45 miners in Six Bells Colliery near Aberbeeg in Wales.

The House of Windsor continued as the family name with The Queen's accession in 1952. Philip retorted, "I am the only man in the country not allowed to give his name to his children." In 1960 The Queen announced that her direct descendants without the title prince or princess would be called Mountbatten-Windsor.

The Christmas Speech this year emphasised that each person is important and although our contribution or influence may be small, it is real and important.

Royal Mail commemorative stamp 2012
Portrait taken from a £1 banknote first issued 1960

Christmas stamp 1960
Behold I bring you good tidings of great joy

Although the contribution which any one person can make is small, it is real and important.

Whether you live in one of the rapidly developing countries of the Commonwealth or whether you find yourself in one of the older countries, the work of mutual help and the increase of mutual understanding cannot fail to be personally satisfying and of real service to the future.

May the months ahead bring you joy and the peace and happiness which we so much desire.

Happy Christmas. God bless you all.

1961

The Queen reflected on her travels and appreciated seeing *"the great volume of good will and friendship that exists between all the varied peoples who profess different faiths and who make up our Commonwealth family."*

Royal visits included a six-week tour of India, Pakistan, Nepal and Iran, from January to early March, visiting the Taj Mahal and laying a wreath on Mahatma Gandhi's monument. There was a state visit to Italy and the Vatican City, calling on Pope John XXIII in May, a state visit to Liberia in November, and visiting Ghana, Sierra Leone and Gambia early in December.

The Queen consults regularly with church leaders, especially the Archbishop of Canterbury. She is deeply involved in planning services for commemorative events and royal weddings, christenings and funerals. Like her coronation, many official commemorations are held in the stately Westminster Abbey. Elizabeth II regularly attends Sunday services and sometimes drives herself to Sandringham Church, entering quietly through a side door to join the congregation. She invites clergy to lunch every Sunday in her winter break at Balmoral in Scotland during January.

This Christmas Speech referred to the carol, *It Came upon the Midnight Clear:* *"Oh hush the noise, ye men of strife, and hear the angels sing."*

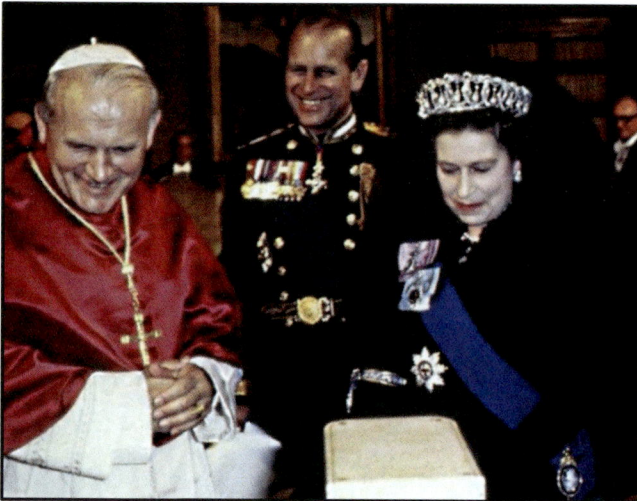

Royal visit to the Vatican City

Christmas stamp 1961
Glory to God in the highest and on earth peace

Every year at this time the whole Christian world celebrates the birth of the founder of our faith. It is traditionally the time for family reunions, present-giving and children's parties.

A welcome escape, in fact, from the harsh realities of this troubled world and it is just in times like these, times of tension and anxieties, that the simple story and message of Christmas is most relevant.

The story is of a poor man and his wife who took refuge at night in a stable, where a child was born and laid in the manger. Nothing very spectacular, and yet the event was greeted with that triumphant song: "Glory to God in the highest, and on earth peace, goodwill towards men."

For that child was to show that there is nothing in heaven and earth that cannot be achieved by faith and by love and service to one's neighbour. Christmas may be a Christian festival, but its message goes out to all men and it is echoed by all men of understanding and goodwill everywhere. ...

"Oh hush the noise, ye men of strife, and hear the angels sing." The words of this old carol mean even more today than when they were first written.

1962

The speech from Buckingham Palace referred to recent successes in space, including the launch of **Telstar**, making it possible to broadcast television, images, and news around the world almost instantly. This message marked the 10th Anniversary of The Queen's first Christmas Message.

Prince Philip opened the 7th British Empire and Commonwealth Games in Perth, Australia, held from 22 November to 1 December, with 35 nations participating.

This year was the 30th Anniversary of the first Christmas Broadcast given by King George V, The Queen's grandfather, on the newly created BBC international service. Rudyard Kipling wrote the speech for the king:

Through one of the marvels of modern Science, I am enabled, this Christmas Day, to speak to all my peoples throughout the Empire. I take it as a good omen that Wireless should have reached its present perfection at a time when the Empire has been linked in closer union. For it offers us immense possibilities to make that union closer still. ...

I speak now from my home and from my heart to you all. To men and women so cut off by the snows, the desert or the sea, that only voices out of the air can reach them; to those cut off from fuller life by blindness, sickness, or infirmity; and to those who are celebrating this day with their children and grand-children. To all—to each—I wish a Happy Christmas. God Bless You!

King George VI, The Queen's father, continued broadcasting annually at Christmas from the outbreak of war in 1939. He concluded his 1942 wartime broadcast, saying:

A former President of the United States of America used to tell the story of a boy who was carrying an even smaller child up a hill. Asked whether the heavy burden was not too much for him, the boy answered, "It's not a burden, it's my brother!" So let us welcome the future in a spirit of brotherhood, and thus make a world in which, please God, all may dwell together in justice and peace.

This year The Queen reflected on how *"these old familiar warm-hearted words of the traditional Christmas message never seem to grow stale."*

Christmas stamp 1962
Early 16th century Spanish carving

A merry Christmas and a happy New Year.

There is something wonderful in the way these old familiar warm-hearted words of the traditional Christmas message never seem to grow stale. Surely it is because the family festival is like a firm landmark in the stormy seas of modern life. ...

Following a star has many meanings; it can mean the religious man's approach to God or the hopes of parents for their children, or the ambition of young men and women, or the devotion of old countries like ours to well-tried ideals of toleration and justice, with no distinction of race or creed.

The wise men of old followed a star: modern man has built one. But unless the message of this new star is the same as theirs our wisdom will count for nought. Now we can all say the world is my neighbour and it is only in serving one another that we can reach for the stars.

God bless you all.

1963

The Queen spoke by radio, being pregnant with her fourth child, **Prince Edward, born in March the following year.** She spoke about the campaign to free the world from hunger and the generous response of Commonwealth nations, and she looked forward to the hope and promise of the future and the need for humanity to be ambitious for all that is good and honourable.

The Royal couple flew via Canada to Fiji, New Zealand and Australia in February.

On 22 November, C S Lewis, the famous Christian author and scholar, died in Oxford and President John F Kennedy was assassinated in America.

In this year's Speech The Queen observed how **the message of Christmas remains the same but needs determination and concerted effort to see it fulfilled.**

Royal Visit, Australian commemorative stamps

Christmas stamp 1963

The message of Christmas remains the same; but humanity can only progress if we are all truly ambitious for what is good and honourable. We know the reward is peace on earth, goodwill toward men, but we cannot win it without determination and concerted effort. ...

Much has been achieved but there is still much to do and on this day of reunions and festivities in the glow of Christmas, let us remember the many undernourished people, young and old, scattered throughout the world.

All my family joins me in sending every one of you best wishes for Christmas and may God's blessing be with you in the coming year.

1964

Queen Elizabeth addressed the important role of the Commonwealth in a year in which anti-apartheid leader **Nelson Mandela** was jailed in **South Africa** and **Indian Prime Minister Jawaharlal Nehru** died.

Prince Edward, Earl of Wessex, The Queen and Prince Philip's third son was born on 10 March, 1964.

The Queen and her husband, The Duke of Edinburgh, visited Canada in October.

In her speech, The Queen expressed appreciation for opportunities to hear about challenges facing her prime ministers in the Commonwealth and spoke about change, alluding to family life with her sailor husband, saying:

All of us who have been blessed with young families know from long experience that when one's house is at its noisiest, there is often less cause for anxiety. The creaking of a ship in a heavy sea is music in the ears of the captain on the bridge. In fact little is static, and without movement there can be no progress.

Royal Mail commemorative stamp 1964
400th Anniversary of Shakespeare's birth

Christmas stamp 1964

To you all, my family and I send our affectionate greetings and hope that your Christmas is a happy one. ...

Some speak today as though the age of adventure and initiative is past. On the contrary, never have the challenges been greater or more urgent. The fight against poverty, malnutrition and ignorance is harder than ever, and we must do all in our power to see that science is directed towards solving these problems. ...

God bless you and a very, very happy Christmas to you all.

1965

The address from Buckingham Palace had the theme of family, from the individual unit to the family of mankind. The Queen praised the growing practice of voluntary service:

A new army is on the march which holds out the brightest hopes for all mankind. It serves in international work camps, in areas hit by natural disasters or emergencies and in helping the poor, the backward or the hungry.

State visits included Ethiopia and Sudan in February and West Germany and West Berlin in May.

This year marked the Golden Jubilee of ANZAC, the Australia and New Zealand Army Corp. Commemorative postage stamps depicted John Simpson Kirkpatrick, a stretcher bearer with the 1st Australian Division in Gallipoli in World War I. After landing at Anzac Cove on 25 April 1915, Simpson used donkeys to carry wounded soldiers to the beach, for evacuation. He did this, often under fire, for three and a half weeks, until he was killed.

This Speech reminded us that Christmas proclaims peace on earth and goodwill towards men.

Australia and New Zealand Army Corp
Golden Jubilee stamp, 1965

Christmas stamp 1965

Every year the familiar pattern of Christmas unfolds. The sights and the customs and festivities may seem very much the same from one year to another, and yet to families and individuals each Christmas is slightly different.

Children grow and presents for them change. It may be the first Christmas for many as husband and wife, or the first Christmas with grandchildren. Some may be far from home, and others lonely or sick, yet Christmas always remains as the great family festival.

A festival which we owe to that family long ago which spent this time in extreme adversity and discomfort. ...

At Christmas we are also reminded that it is the time of peace on earth and goodwill towards men. Yet we are all only too well aware of the tragic fighting, hatred and ill-will in so many parts of the world. ...

"Peace on Earth" - we may not have it at the moment, we may never have it completely, but we will certainly achieve nothing unless we go on trying to remove the causes of conflict between peoples and nations.

"Goodwill towards men" is not a hollow phrase. Goodwill exists, and when there is an opportunity to show it in practical form we know what wonderful things it can achieve.

1966

The Queen spoke about the increasingly prominent and important role played by women in society:

The devotion of nuns and nurses, the care of mothers and wives, the service of teachers, and the conviction of reformers are the real and enduring presents which women have always given.

The Royal Visit to the West Indies in February included Barbados, British Guiana, Trinidad, Tobago, Grenada, St. Vincent, St. Lucia, Domini, Montserrat, Antigua, St. Kitts, Nevis, British Virgin Islands, and the Bahamas in February, and Jamaica in March. Belgium had the state visit in May. The 8th British and Commonwealth Games were held in Kingston, Jamaica, 4-13 August, with 34 nations participating.

The only time England won the FIFA World Cup soccer was in July 1966 at Wembley Stadium, London.

Australia adopted decimal currency on Valentine's Day, 14 February, introducing colourful notes and coins.

This Christmas Speech focused on concern for others, as in giving presents.

Australian pound and dollar currency, 1966

Christmas stamp 1966
Emmanuel – God with us

Ever since the first Christmas when the wise men brought their presents, Christians all over the world have kept up this kindly custom.

Even if the presents we give each other at Christmas-time may only be intended to give momentary pleasure, they do also reflect one all important lesson. Society cannot hope for a just and peaceful civilisation unless each individual feels the need to be concerned about his fellows.

... I am sure the custom of giving presents at Christmas will never die out, but I hope it will never overshadow the far more important presents we can give for the benefit of the future of the world.

People of goodwill everywhere are working to build a world that will be a happier and more peaceful place in which to live. Let our prayers be for a personal strength and conviction to play our own small part to bring that day nearer.

God be with you, and a very happy Christmas to you all.

1967

Queen Elizabeth spoke about Canada's centenary of its confederation and mentioned the knighting of Sir Francis Chichester, the first man to sail solo around the world. This message, filmed at Buckingham Palace, the first in colour, noted modern communications and the timeless Christmas message.

The Queen and Duke of Edinburgh toured Canada in June and July for the Centennial celebrations and the EXPO at Montreal. They returned to Malta in November, celebrating the 20th Anniversary of their wedding. Their honeymoon took them to Malta where Prince Philip had been stationed on the island as a naval officer

This year was also the 20th Anniversary of the radio broadcast the then Princess Elizabeth made from South Africa on her 21st birthday while touring with her parents King George VI and Queen Elizabeth and her sister Princess Margaret. She concluded that broadcast with these words:

I declare before you all that my whole life whether it be long or short shall be devoted to your service and the service of our great imperial family to which we all belong.

But I shall not have strength to carry out this resolution alone unless you join in it with me, as I now invite you to do: I know that your support will be unfailingly given. God help me to make good my vow, and God bless all of you who are willing to share in it.

Christmas stamps 1967

The first Royal Christmas Message televised in colour

Modern communications make it possible for me to talk to you in your homes and to wish you a merry Christmas and a very happy New Year. These techniques of radio and television are modern, but the Christmas message is timeless.

You may have heard it very often but in the end, no matter what scientific progress we make, the message will count for nothing unless we can achieve real peace and encourage genuine goodwill between individual people and the nations of the world.

Every Christmas I am sustained and encouraged by the happiness and sense of unity which comes from seeing all the members of my family together.

I hope and pray that, with God's help, this Christmas spirit of family unity will spread and grow among our Commonwealth family of nations.

1968

This year's Christmas message came from Buckingham Palace and had the theme of brotherhood in this year of the Baptist minister and civil rights leader Martin Luther King Jr.'s assassination in April.

State visits were made to Brazil and Chile in November.

The Queen observed:

Every individual and every nation have problems, so there is all the more reason for us to do our utmost to show our concern for others.

Martin Luther King Jr.

Christmas stamp 1968
O come all ye faithful
Joyful and triumphant

Christmas is a Christian festival which celebrates the birth of the Prince of Peace. At times it is almost hidden by the merry making and tinsel, but the essential message of Christmas is still that we all belong to the great brotherhood of man.

This idea is not limited to the Christian faith. Philosophers and prophets have concluded that peace is better than war, love is better than hate and that mankind can only find progress in friendship and co-operation.

Many ideas are being questioned today, but these great truths will continue to shine out as the light of hope in the darkness of intolerance and inhumanity. ...

Christmas is the festival of peace. It is God's will that it should be our constant endeavour to establish 'Peace on earth, goodwill towards men'.

I hope you all have a very happy Christmas and every good fortune in the New Year.

1969

There was no Christmas Broadcast in 1969 because a special documentary film, 'Royal Family', had been made in connection with the Investiture of The Prince of Wales on 1 July. The Queen issued a written message instead, and said:

I have received a great number of kind letters and messages of regard and concern about this year's break with the usual broadcast at Christmas and I want you all to know that my good wishes are no less warm and personal because they come to you in a different form.

She was pleased that her older children were entering the service of the country and the Commonwealth and stated that she looked forward to her visit the next year to Australia and New Zealand for the Cook Bi-centenary and to Fiji, Tonga and northern Canada. There was a state visit to Austria in May this year.

The Queen's message mentioned the end of the 1960s and the decade's significance including it being the time when men first walked on the moon. Neil Armstrong and Buzz Aldrin, landed the lunar module *Eagle* on 20 July 20, 1969. Armstrong stepped onto the moon on 21 July, six hours after landing, saying, "That's one small step for man. One giant leap for mankind." Aldrin joined him 20 minutes later. Michael Collins piloted the command module *Columbia* in lunar orbit while they were on the Moon's surface.

Moon walk, 21 July, 1969, NASA

Christmas stamps 1969

It is only natural that we should all be dazzled and impressed by the triumphs of technology, but Christmas is a festival of the spirit. At this time our concern is particularly for the lonely, the sick and the elderly. I hope they will all feel the warmth and comfort of companionship and that all of you will enjoy a very happy Christmas with your families and friends.

God bless you all.

1970

Televised again, The Queen's Speech recounted some of the trips she made during the year and included film shot in **Australia**, New Zealand and Canada.

The Duke of Edinburgh opened and The Queen closed the renamed 9th British Commonwealth Games, held in Edinburgh, Scotland, from 16 to 25 July with 42 nations participating. Metric units and electronic photo-finish technology were used for the first time and the Games were followed by the Commonwealth Paraplegic Games for wheelchair athletes.

In 1970 The Queen became the first Sovereign to inaugurate and address the General Synod of the Church of England.

Royal tours this year included Canada, Fiji, Tonga, and New Zealand in March, Australia in April, and Canada in May and July. This year **marked the 200th anniversary of the voyage of Captain Cook sighting Australia and claiming its allegiance to Britain.**

The royal walkabout is now familiar after nearly half a century. The first royal walkabout is reported to have been in 1970 during the official tour of Australia and New Zealand, hence the use of the name from the Aboriginal custom of walkabout. It gives ordinary people, not just officials, opportunity to meet the Royal Family informally and it became very popular. The Queen once famously quipped, "I have to be seen to be believed."

This year The Queen referred again to the importance of the Commonwealth and how the Christmas message is about being concerned for one another.

Australian commemorative 50 cent coin, 1970
with Elizabeth II and James Cook

Christmas stamp 1970

The strength of the Commonwealth lies in its history and the way people feel about it. All those years through which we have lived together have given us an exchange of people and ideas which ensures that there is a continuing concern for each other.

That, very simply, is the message of Christmas - learning to be concerned about one another; to treat your neighbour as you would like him to treat you; and to care about the future of all life on earth.

These matters of the spirit are more important and more lasting than simple material development. It is a hard lesson, but I think that we in the Commonwealth have perhaps begun to understand it.

I wish you all a merry Christmas. God bless you all.

1971

Focusing on the theme of families, the television version showed Prince Andrew and Prince Edward looking at a family photograph album.

The Commonwealth Heads of Government Meeting (CHOGM), a biennial summit meeting of the heads of government from all Commonwealth nations, began in January 1971 in Singapore. Every two years the meeting is held in a different member state, chaired by that nation's respective Prime Minister or President. Queen Elizabeth, the Head of the Commonwealth, attended every CHOGM from 1973 in Ottawa, Canada, until 2011 in Perth, Australia. Her formal participation began in 1997. Prince Charles represented her at the 2013 meeting in Sri Lanka because the 87-year-old monarch was curtailing her overseas travel. She continued to attend CHOGMs held in Europe and was present at the 2015 summit in Malta and is expected to attend the 2018 CHOGM to be held in London.

The Queen and her husband toured Canada in May, and made a state visit to Turkey in October.

The Speech this year emphasised that *"The Christmas message is really one for all seasons and not just for one day of the year."*

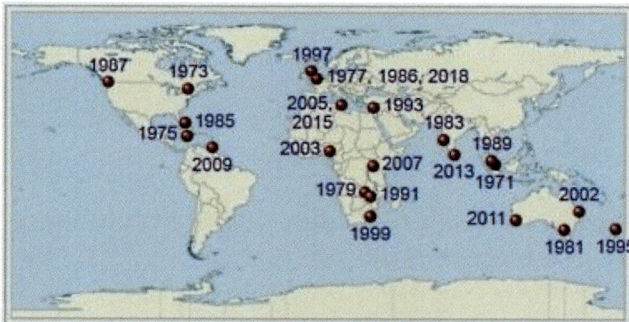

25 CHOGM gatherings hosted by 17 countries in 22 cities

Christmas stamp 1971
3 kings follow the star

Christmas is the time for families and for children, and it's also a time when we realise that another year is coming to an end.

As the familiar pattern of Christmas and the New Year repeats itself, we may sometimes forget how much the world about us has been changing.

... Many of you who are listening are able, like me, to enjoy this Christmas with your families, and your children can enjoy the day as all children should. But tragically, there are many millions of others for whom this cannot be the same. Our thoughts and prayers should be for them. ...

The Christmas message is really one for all seasons and not just for one day of the year. If we can show this by our lives and by our example, then our contribution as parents will be just as important as any made by scientists and engineers.

Perhaps we can then look for the real peace on earth, and the powers which men have harnessed will be used for the benefit of our fellow men.

I hope this Christmas Day is bringing to many of you peace and happiness, and for everyone the hope of this to come. May God bless you all.

1972

The television broadcast this year included scenes from the celebration of The Queen's Silver Wedding celebrating 25 years of marriage to The Duke of Edinburgh. Royal visits this year included visits to Singapore, Malaysia, Brunei, Seychelles, Mauritius and Kenya in February and March. There were state visits to Thailand in February, Maldives in March, France in May and Yugoslavia in October.

In her broadcast Queen Elizabeth mentioned the violence in **Northern Ireland**, as well as the preparations for Britain to join the **European Economic Community**. She praised **voluntary workers** who have *"struggled to keep humanity and commonsense alive"* and acknowledged the excellent work of the social services and the forces of law and order doing *"their thankless task with the utmost fortitude."*

On 18 May The Queen and Prince Philip, together with Prince Charles, visited The Duke of Windsor's home in the Bois de Boulogne in Paris. The Queen spent fifteen minutes alone with her uncle The Duke of Windsor. He died ten days later, on 28 May. After his funeral service in St George's Chapel, Windsor, the Duke's body was buried in the royal burial ground at Frogmore, where, fourteen years later, the Duchess of Windsor's body was also buried. The Duke of Windsor, formerly King Edward VIII, had reigned from **20 January 1936** until his abdication on **11 December 1936**, the year of the three kings, George V, Edward VIII, and George VI.

The Queen's Christmas Message spoke of new life and the old message.

George V, Edward VIII, George VI, Australian stamps 1936-1937

Christmas stamps 1972
Jesus friend of children and
Christ the Light of the world

Christmas is above all a time of new life. A time to look hopefully ahead to a future when the problems which face the world today will be seen in their true perspective.

I leave with you the old message, "On earth peace; goodwill toward men". No one has ever offered a better formula and I hope that its simple truth may yet take hold of the imagination of all mankind.

God bless you and a happy Christmas to you all.

1973

The Queen's Speech this year included **film shot at Buckingham Palace on the wedding day of** The Queen's daughter, **Princess Anne** to Captain **Mark Phillips**.

The Queen again visited Canada in June and July, returning for the Heads of Commonwealth meeting in Ottawa in August. During October she visited Fiji and then Australia for the opening of the Opera House in Sydney.

This year The Queen reminded us that *"Christ taught love and charity and that we should show humanity and compassion at all times and in all situations"* and that Christmas is especially a *"festival of tolerance and companionship."*

Sydney Opera House
with Sydney Harbour Bridge

Christmas stamps 1973
This is my Beloved Son and
I am the Good Shepherd

I believe that Christmas should remind us that the qualities of the human spirit are more important than material gain. Christ taught love and charity and that we should show humanity and compassion at all times and in all situations.

A lack of humanity and compassion can be very destructive - how easily this causes diversions within nations and between nations. We should remember instead how much we have in common and resolve to give expression to the best of our human qualities, not only at Christmas, but right through the year.

In this Christmas spirit let us greet all our fellow men and join together in this festival of tolerance and companionship.

I wish you all a very happy Christmas.

1974

Until 1974 the Royal Family gathered at Sandringham for Christmas, but after that year the growing family gathered at Windsor Castle, where they traditionally gather for Easter. Since 1988, when the castle was being rewired, Royal Christmases returned to Sandringham.

In January The Queen and Prince Philip visited the Cook Islands to open the Rarotonga International Airport, and in February visited New Zealand for the Commonwealth Games and then Norfolk Island, New Hebrides (now Vanuatu), British Solomon Islands, Papua New Guinea and Australia. They had a state visit to Indonesia in March.

The 10th British Commonwealth Games held in Christchurch, New Zealand, with 38 nations participating from 24 January to 2 February, were officially named "the friendly games". The Games were held after the 1974 Commonwealth Paraplegic Games in Dunedin for wheelchair athletes.

The purposely built QEII Park was later severely damaged by the devastating earthquake that destroyed parts of Christchurch on 22 February 2011.

In her Christmas Speech The Queen spoke about opening Parliaments a record four times this year, in New Zealand, in Australia and twice in Westminster.

This year's Christmas message referred to problems such as the continuing violence in Northern Ireland and the **Middle East**, the **famine in Bangladesh**, and the **floods in Brisbane, Australia**.

Amid the darkness there is hope: *"The first Christmas came at a time that was dark and threatening, but from it came the light of the world."*

Christmas stamps 1974
Adoration of the Kings and the Flight to Egypt

You may be asking what can we do personally to make things better?

I believe the Christmas message provides the best clue. Goodwill is better than resentment, tolerance is better than revenge, compassion is better than anger, above all a lively concern for the interests of others as well as our own.

In times of doubt and anxiety the attitudes people show in their daily lives, in their homes, and in their work, are of supreme importance.

It is by acting in this spirit that every man, woman and child can help and 'make a difference'. ...

My message today is one of encouragement and hope.

Christmas on this side of the equator comes at the darkest time of the year: but we can look forward hopefully to lengthening days and the returning sun.

The first Christmas came at a time that was dark and threatening, but from it came the light of the world.

I wish you all a happy Christmas.

1975

Broadcast from the gardens of Buckingham Palace, this was the first time the message had been recorded outdoors. The Speech referred to problems associated with a year of record inflation and unemployment in the United Kingdom and worldwide.

The Queen visited Bermuda, Barbados and the Bahamas in February, Kingston Jamaica for the Heads of Commonwealth Conference in April, and Hong Kong in May.

State visits included Mexico in March and Japan in May.

The Queen's Speech emphasized that small acts can make a big difference like ripples spreading in a pond from a small stone, or like enough grains of sand on one side of scales:

Like those grains of sand, they can tip the balance. So take heart from the Christmas message and be happy.

Christmas stamp 1975

Christmas Broadcast 1975

Christmas is a festival which brings us together in small groups, a family group if we are lucky. Today we are not just nameless people in a crowd. We meet as friends who are glad to be together and who care about each other's happiness. ...

For most of us - I wish it could be for everyone - this is a holiday, and I think it's worth reminding ourselves why. We are celebrating a birthday - the birthday of a child born nearly 2,000 years ago, who grew up and lived for only about 30 years.

That one person, by his example and by his revelation of the good which is in us all, has made an enormous difference to the lives of people who have come to understand his teaching. His simple message of love has been turning the world upside down ever since. He showed that what people are and what they do, does matter and does make all the difference.

He commanded us to love our neighbours as we love ourselves, but what exactly is meant by 'loving ourselves'? I believe it means trying to make the most of the abilities we have been given, it means caring for our talents.

It is a matter of making the best of ourselves, not just doing the best for ourselves.

1976

To mark the **United States Bicentennial**, The Queen and The Duke of Edinburgh undertook a state visit to the United States of America. That visit, and the theme of reconciliation after disagreements, formed the focus of this year's Christmas Broadcast.

Recalling how the long drought of England's summer gave way to rapid flowering when the rains came, The Queen likened that to the way peace can blossom after conflict ceases.

The Queen's travels took her and her husband to Canada and America in July for the Olympic Games in Montreal, and for the American Bicentennial. State visits also included Finland in May, and Luxembourg in November.

"Christmas is a time for reconciliation," **The Queen reminded us.**

The Queen, President Gerald Ford, and Prince Philip
The United States of America Bicentennial

Christmas stamp 1976

Christmas is a time for reconciliation. A time not only for families and friends to come together but also for differences to be forgotten. ...

Reconciliation, like the one that followed the American War of Independence, is the product of reason, tolerance and love, and I think that Christmas is a good time to reflect on it. ...

The gift I would most value next year is that reconciliation should be found wherever it is needed. A reconciliation which would bring peace and security to families and neighbours at present suffering and torn apart.

Remember that good spreads outwards and every little does help. Mighty things from small beginnings grow as indeed they grew from the small child of Bethlehem. ...

I wish you all a very happy Christmas and may the New Year bring reconciliation between all people.

1977

The Queen recalled **her Silver Jubilee celebrations**, commemorating 25 years of her reign. She expressed her hope for reconciliation in Northern Ireland, which she visited in August for the first time in 11 years.

During summer, The Queen embarked on a large-scale tour of the country, with six jubilee tours in Britain and Northern Ireland covering 36 counties in three months. Her visit to Hillsborough Castle in Ireland included her first arrival by helicopter.

Official overseas visits in 12 Commonwealth countries included Western Samoa, Tonga, Fiji and New Zealand in February, Australia and Papua New Guinea in March, then Canada and the West Indies nations of the Bahamas, British Virgin Islands, Antigua, Barbuda, and Barbados in October, ending with a flight back to London on the supersonic passenger aircraft Concorde.

Her Majesty thanked the people of the Commonwealth for their warm reception and their generous support of **the Silver Jubilee Appeal, raising funds to support young people and, in particular, to help young people help others.**

The Queen expressed her hope that the Christian spirit of reconciliation would continue to burn strongly in our hearts.

Elizabeth II Silver Jubilee, Crown Medal Appeal

Christmas stamp 1977

Last Christmas I said that my wish for 1977 was that it should be a year of reconciliation. You have shown by the way in which you have celebrated the Jubilee that this was not an impossible dream. Thank you all for your response. ...

The Jubilee celebrations in London started with a Service of Thanksgiving in St. Paul's Cathedral. To me this was a thanksgiving for all the good things for which our Commonwealth stands - the comradeship and co-operation it inspires and the friendship and tolerance it encourages. These are the qualities needed by all mankind.

The evening before the Service I lit one small flame at Windsor and a chain of bonfires spread throughout Britain and on across the world to New Zealand and Australia.

My hope this Christmas is that the Christian spirit of reconciliation may burn as strongly in our hearts during the coming year.

God bless you and a very happy Christmas to you all.

1978

The future was the subject of this broadcast showing footage of The Queen with her new grandson, **Peter Phillips**, and Princess Anne, as well as recordings replayed from earlier broadcasts by The Queen's grandfather George V, her father George VI, and from her own first broadcast in 1952 and her first television broadcast in 1957.

State visits were made to West Germany and West Berlin in May.

The permanently renamed Commonwealth Games were held in Edmonton, Canada from 3 to 12 August with 47 nations participating. These 11th Commonwealth Games were the first to use a computerised system for ticket sales. The Queen and Prince Philip were involved with their sons Prince Andrew and Prince Edward during their royal tour of Canada, 26 July to 6 August.

This Christmas Broadcast reminded us: *"The birth of Christ gave us faith in the future,"* and *"the optimism of that Christmas message is timeless"* and we have *"the compelling example of the life and teaching of Christ".*

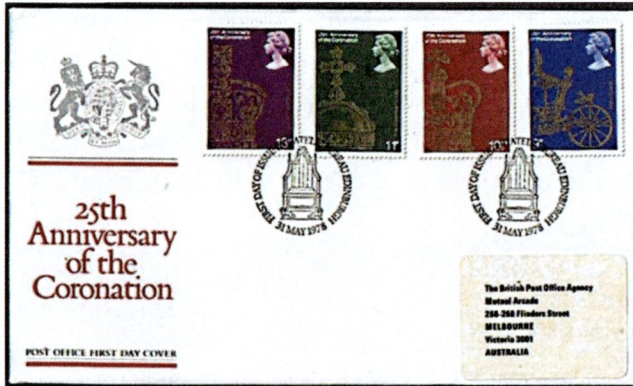

Royal Mail commemorative stamps
25th Anniversary of the Coronation

Christmas stamps 1978
after Van Eyck: *The Madonna & the Child*
Marmion: *The Virgin & Child*
del Vaga: *The Holy Family*

At Christmas, we look back nearly 2000 years to an event which was to bring new hope and new confidence to all subsequent generations.

The birth of Christ gave us faith in the future and as I read through some earlier Christmas Broadcasts, I was struck by the way that this same idea - faith in the future - kept recurring. ...

The optimism of that Christmas message is timeless. When it first fell to me to carry on the tradition that my grandfather and father had developed, I reaffirmed what I knew had been their deeply held beliefs in the future, beliefs which I myself share. ...

Christians have the compelling example of the life and teaching of Christ and, for myself, I would like nothing more than that my grandchildren should hold dear his ideals which have helped and inspired so many previous generations.

I wish you all, together with your children and grandchildren, a very happy Christmas.

1979

This Christmas message addressed the theme of children and young people in this International Year of the Child. The Queen appreciated the Commonwealth's support for children including volunteers working for the Save the Children Fund, with Princess Anne its President. **Ceefax** was used for the first time in this broadcast, providing subtitles for the hard of hearing.

Royal Tours in July and August included Tanzania, Malawi, Botswana and then Lusaka in Zambia for the Commonwealth Heads of Government Meeting held 1-7 August with the full 39 member nations represented.

State visits included visiting Kuwait, Bahrain, Saudi Arabia, Qatar, United Arab Emirates and Oman in February-March and Denmark in May.

On 27 August 1979, Lord Louis Mountbatten, his grandson Nicholas and two others were killed by an IRA bomb hidden on his fishing boat in Donegal Bay, Northern Ireland. Later that day, an IRA bomb killed 18 British paratroopers in County Down, Northern Ireland. Lord Mountbatten, an uncle of Prince Philip and second cousin of The Queen, **was the last Viceroy of India (1947) and the first Governor-General of independent India (1947–48).**

This year hundreds of thousands of refugees fled Cambodia during the disastrous rule of the Khmer Rouge.

The Christmas Broadcast noted that *"we celebrate the birth of the child who transformed history and gave us a great faith."*

Indian commemorative stamp 1980
Mountbatten 1900-1979

Christmas stamps 1979
Eastern European Icon: *Christ's Nativity*
International gifts
Buglioni: *Madonna and Child*

At Christmas we give presents to each other. Let us also stop to think whether we are making enough effort to pass on our experience of life to our children. Today we celebrate the birth of the child who transformed history and gave us a great faith. Jesus said:

"Suffer the little children to come unto me and forbid them not, for of such is the kingdom of God".

I wish you all a very happy Christmas.

1980

This message attracted a record 28 million viewers in the United Kingdom, and millions more worldwide. It reflected on the celebrations of the 80th birthday of **Queen Elizabeth, The Queen Mother and** addressed the theme of service in its many forms. The Royal couple visited Australia in May.

State visits were made to Switzerland in April-May, and Italy, the Vatican City, Tunisia, Algeria and Morocco in October.

The Queen began her message with these words:

I was glad that the celebrations of my mother's 80th birthday last summer gave so much pleasure. I wonder whether you remember, during the Thanksgiving Service in St. Paul's, the congregation singing that wonderful hymn "Immortal, Invisible, God only wise".

"Now give us we pray thee the Spirit of love,
The gift of true wisdom that comes from above,
The spirit of service that has naught of pride,
The gift of true courage, and thee as our guide."

This Christmas Speech concluded with these words:

When you hear the bells ringing at Christmas, think of the lines written by Tennyson:

"Ring out false pride in place and blood,
The civic slander and the spite;
Ring in the love of truth and right,
Ring in the common love of good ...

Ring in the valiant man and free,
The larger heart, the kindlier hand,
Ring out the darkness of the land,
Ring in the Christ that is to be."

Christmas stamps 1980
Prospero Fontana: *Holy Family*
School of M. Zuern: *Madonna and Child*

In difficult times we may be tempted to find excuses for self-indulgence and to wash our hands of responsibility. Christmas stands for the opposite. The Wise Men and the Shepherds remind us that it is not enough simply to do our jobs; we need to go out and look for opportunities to help those less fortunate than ourselves, even if that service demands sacrifice.

It was their belief and confidence in God which inspired them to visit the stable and it is this unselfish will to serve that will see us through the difficulties we face.

We know that the world can never be free from conflict and pain, but Christmas also draws our attention to all that is hopeful and good in this changing world; it speaks of values and qualities that are true and permanent and it reminds us that the world we would like to see can only come from the goodness of the heart. ...

To all of you, wherever you may be, I wish happiness this Christmas.

1981

This Speech, broadcast from the terrace of Buckingham Palace overlooking the garden, focused on service to disabled people in this **International Year of Disabled Persons.** Over 750 million viewers watched the royal wedding of Prince Charles to Princess Diana on 29 July in Westminster Abbey.

On 14 June, a few weeks before the wedding, six shots, all blanks, disturbed the Trooping of the Colour. The Queen quickly calmed her horse, named Burmese, which she **rode for 18 years from 1969 until 1986 for her 60th birthday parade, after which the horse retired. Since then Her Majesty has ridden in Queen Victoria's phaeton carriage for the birthday parade.**

Royal tours included Australia in September for the Commonwealth Heads of Government Meeting in Melbourne and New Zealand and Sri Lanka in October. The state visit to Norway was in May.

Australian Christmas postage stamps in 1981 used these words from obscure Australian carols, including the first verse of **'Christmas Bush for His Adorning,'** and the second stanza of **'The Silver Stars are in the Sky,'** with lyrics by John Wheeler and music by William James:

All the bells are gaily ringing	Once long ago, against her breast
Birds in ev'ry tree are singing	A mother rocked her child to rest
Let us in this golden weather	Who was the Prince of Heav'n above
Gather Christmas bush together	The Lord of happiness and love

Royal Mail commemorative stamp
Prince Charles and Lady Diana Spencer

Christmas stamps 1981

As human beings we generally know what is right and how we should act and speak. But we are also very aware of how difficult it is to have the courage of our convictions.

Our Christian faith helps us to sustain those convictions. Christ not only revealed to us the truth in his teachings. He lived by what he believed and gave us the strength to try to do the same - and, finally, on the cross, he showed the supreme example of physical and moral courage.

That sacrifice was the dawn of Christianity and this is why at Christmas time we are inspired by the example of Christ as we celebrate his birth.

A few weeks ago I was sent this poem:

"When all your world is torn with grief and strife
Think yet - when there seems nothing left to mend
The frail and time-worn fabric of your life,
The golden thread of courage has no end."

So to you all I say - God bless you, and a very happy Christmas.

1982

Marking the 50th anniversary of the first Christmas Broadcast, The Queen delivered this year's Speech in the library of **Windsor Castle**, for the first time. The theme was "the sea", in a year in which British troops fought in the **Falklands War** in the **South Atlantic Ocean**. This year saw the birth and christening of The Queen's third grandchild **Prince William, an heir to the throne.**

In July an intruder broke into The Queen's bedroom in Buckingham Palace. Her Majesty, skilled at talking to strangers, conversed with him until astonished staff arrived to rescue her.

Royal tours included Canada in April, then Australia for the Commonwealth Games in October, and on to Papua New Guinea, the Solomon Islands, Nauru, Kiribati, Tuvalu and Fiji in October. In Australia, with its "G'day mate" egalitarian culture, 46 nations participated in the 12th Commonwealth Games in Brisbane, officially opened by The Duke of Edinburgh and closed by The Queen, who reflected on the Games in her Christmas Speech:

Any of you who attended or watched the events at the Commonwealth Games at Brisbane cannot have failed to notice the unique atmosphere of friendly rivalry and the generous applause for all the competitors.

In a world more concerned with argument, disagreement and violence, the Games stand out as a demonstration of the better side of human nature and of the great value of the Commonwealth as an association of free and independent nations.

The Games also illustrated the consequences of the movement of peoples within the Commonwealth. Colour is no longer an indication of national origin. Until this century most racial and religious groups remained concentrated in their homelands but today almost every country of the Commonwealth has become multi-racial and multi-religious.

Christmas stamp 1982

At this time of the year, Christians celebrate the birth of their Saviour, but no longer in an exclusive way. We hope that our greetings at Christmas to all people of religious conviction and goodwill will be received with the same understanding that we try to show in receiving the greetings of other religious groups at their special seasons.

The poet John Donne said: "No man is an island, entire of itself; every man is a piece of the continent, a part of the main." That is the message of the Commonwealth and it is also the Christian message.

Christ attached supreme importance to the individual and he amazed the world in which he lived by making it clear that the unfortunate and the underprivileged had an equal place in the Kingdom of Heaven with the rich and powerful. But he also taught that man must do his best to live in harmony with man and to love his neighbours.

In the Commonwealth, we are all neighbours and it is with this thought in mind that I wish you all, wherever you may be, the blessings of a happy and peaceful Christmas.

1983

This Christmas message discussed new possibilities for co-operation within the Commonwealth of Nations permitted by modern technologies. The Queen mentioned a visit to **Bangladesh** and India that year, in which she met Indian Prime Minister **Indira Gandhi**, invested **Mother Teresa** into the **Order of Merit**, and met with the **Commonwealth Heads of Government** in **New Delhi**, India.

The Queen summarized their travels: *Prince Philip and I were able to visit Jamaica, Mexico, the United States and Canada in the winter, followed by Sweden in the summer, and ending up in the autumn with Kenya, Bangladesh and finally India for the Commonwealth Heads of Government Meeting in New Delhi.*

State visits were to Mexico in February, the United States in February-March, and Sweden in May.

This year's Christmas message discussed the promise and possibilities of nations working together using modern technology to alleviate human need and to help bridge the vast gap between the rich and the poor.

Mother Teresa receiving the Nehru Award
from Indian Prime Minister Indira Gandhi

Christmas stamp 1983

I hope that Christmas will remind us all that it is not how we communicate but what we communicate with each other that really matters.

We in the Commonwealth are fortunate enough to belong to a world wide comradeship. Let us make the most of it; let us all resolve to communicate as friends in tolerance and understanding. Only then can we make the message of the angels come true: 'Peace on earth, goodwill towards men'.

I always look forward to being able to talk to everyone at Christmas time and at the end of another year I again send you all my warmest greetings.

1984

This year's message described how adults could learn from children, with film footage showing the christening of Prince Harry, The Queen's fourth grandchild. It included lively film of big brother Prince William chasing his cousin Zara Phillips around the Archbishop of Canterbury's legs, and Princess Diana explaining to William the many royal generations who had worn the baby's christening robes.

There was a state visit to Jordan in March and The Queen and Prince Philip returned to Canada in September-October.

The Royal Mail in the United Kingdom issued a stamp for the Centenary of Greenwich Meridian, 1884-1984, with a view of the earth from Apollo 11.

The Christmas Speech reminded us that Christmas **marks the birth of the Prince of Peace.**

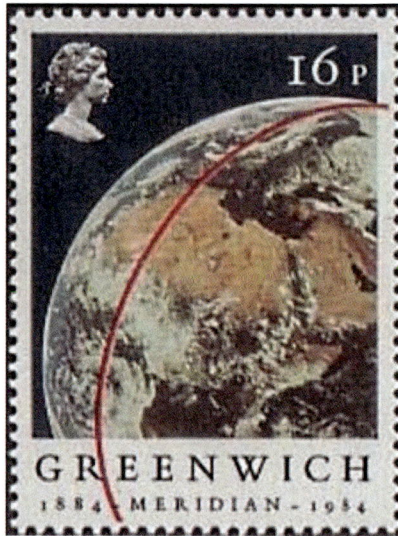

Royal Mail commemorative stamp

Christmas stamps 1984

It is particularly at Christmas, which marks the birth of the Prince of Peace, that we should work to heal old wounds and to abandon prejudice and suspicion.

What better way of making a start than by remembering what Christ said - "Except ye become as little children, ye shall not enter into the Kingdom of Heaven".

God bless you and a very happy Christmas to you all.

1985

The Queen referred to the **earthquake that struck Mexico City**, the **volcanic eruption in Colombia**, famine in Africa, and the **Air India crash off the coast of Ireland**, but her message focused on the good news stories of the year.

Again The Queen praised remarkable public achievements with film footage of some of the annual 2,000 investitures and award presentations for **acts of bravery or recognition for service**. The Speech gave examples of outstanding achievements in a wide range of services and enterprise.

The state visit to Portugal was in March. In October The Queen and Prince Philip visited the Caribbean islands of Belize, the Bahamas for the Commonwealth Heads of Government Meeting, Little Inagua Island, St Kitts-Nevis, Antigua, Dominica, St. Lucia, St. Vincent and the Grenadines, Barbados and Grenada, finishing in Trinidad and Tobago in November.

In spite of prevailing bad news there is still good news everywhere.

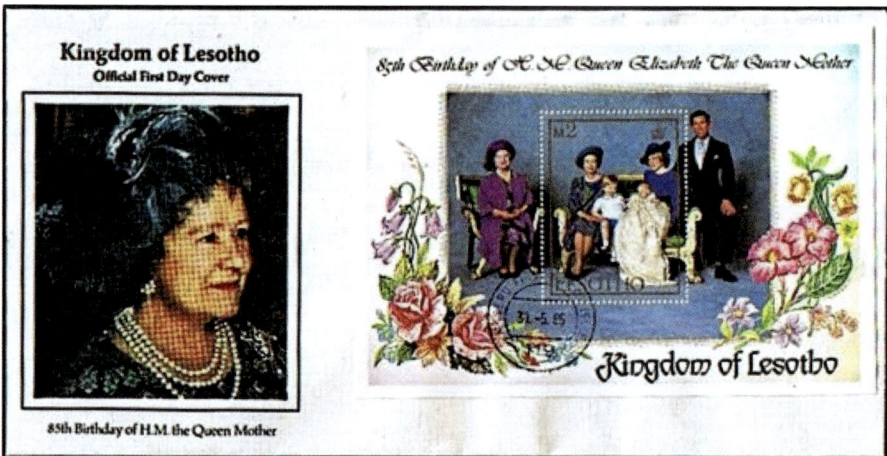

The Queen Mother, 85th birthday
Kingdom of Lesotho commemorative stamps

Christmas stamps 1985

Christmas is a time of good news. I believe it is a time to look at the good things in life and to remember that there are a great many people trying to make the world a better place, even though their efforts may go unrecognised.

There is a lesson in this for us all and we should never forget our obligation to make our own individual contributions, however small, towards the sum of human goodness.

The story of the Good Samaritan reminds us of our duty to our neighbour. We should try to follow Christ's clear instruction at the end of that story: "Go and do thou likewise".

I wish you all a very happy Christmas and I hope that we shall all try to make some good news in the coming year.

1986

Sir David Attenborough produced the Christmas Broadcasts from 1986 to 1991. This one, in the year of The Queen's 60th birthday, filmed in the **Royal Mews** at Buckingham Palace, stressed society's responsibility towards children. Prince Andrew married Sarah Ferguson on 23 July.

David Attenborough admitted in his autobiography *Life On Air* that in 1986 he was "quiveringly nervous". The Queen spoke perfectly but a horse in the background wriggled its itchy lips and David Attenborough later observed that it looked on screen like it was a ventriloquist, so they had to record the segment again. The Queen was amused.

Royal tours included New Zealand in February and Australia in March and October. Only 27 of a possible 59 nations participated in the 13th Commonwealth Games, held for the second time in Edinburgh, Scotland, in July to August, because of boycotts against apartheid in South Africa. The Commonwealth Heads of Government meeting in London (3-5 August) followed the Games. State visits were to Nepal in February and the People's Republic of China in October.

This year The Queen gave longer reflections on the significance of Christmas.

Christmas is a festival for all Christians, but it is particularly a festival for children. As we all know, it commemorates the birth of a child, who was born to ordinary people, and who grew up very simply in his own small home town and was trained to be a carpenter.

His life thus began in humble surroundings, in fact in a stable, but he was to have a profound influence on the course of history, and on the lives of generations of his followers. You don't have to be rich or powerful in order to change things for the better and each of us in our own way can make a contribution.

The infant Jesus was fortunate in one very important respect. His parents were loving and considerate. They did their utmost to protect him from harm. They left their own home and became refugees, to save him from King Herod, and they brought him up according to the traditions of their faith. ...

Christmas stamps 1986

It is no easy task to care for and bring up children, whatever your circumstances - whether you are famous or quite unknown. But we could all help by letting the spirit of Christmas fill our homes with love and care and by heeding Our Lord's injunction to treat others as you would like them to treat you.

When, as the Bible says, Christ grew in wisdom and understanding, he began his task of explaining and teaching just what it is that God wants from us.

The two lessons that he had for us, which he underlined in everything he said and did, are the messages of God's love and how essential it is that we, too, should love other people.

There are many serious and threatening problems in this country and in the world but they will never be solved until there is peace in our homes and love in our hearts.

The message which God sent us by Christ's life and example is a very simple one, even though it seems so difficult to put into practice.

To all of you, of every faith and race, I send you my best wishes for a time of peace and tranquillity with your families at this Festival of Christmas. A very Happy Christmas to you all.

1987

The Queen referred to the **Remembrance Day bombing** in Enniskillen, Northern Ireland, and stressed the importance of tolerance and forgiveness. A peak of 28 million viewers in the United Kingdom tuned into the broadcast and millions more watched and listened throughout the Commonwealth.

There was a state visit to West Germany in May.

The Queen toured Canada in October and attended the Commonwealth Heads of Government Meeting in Vancouver.

The broadcast called for mutual understanding, tolerance, and forgiveness, with examples drawn from this year's violence:

From time to time we also see some inspiring examples of tolerance. Mr Gordon Wilson, whose daughter Marie lost her life in the horrifying explosion at Enniskillen on Remembrance Sunday, impressed the whole world by the depth of his forgiveness.

His strength, and that of his wife, and the courage of their daughter, came from their Christian conviction. All of us will echo their prayer that out of the personal tragedies of Enniskillen may come a reconciliation between the communities.

Remembrance Day

Christmas stamps 1987

There are striking illustrations of the way in which the many different religions can come together in peaceful harmony. Each year I try to attend the Commonwealth Day inter-faith Observance at Westminster Abbey. At that service all are united in their willingness to pray for the common good.

This is a symbol of mutual tolerance and I find it most encouraging. Of course it is right that people should hold their beliefs and their faiths strongly and sincerely, but perhaps we should also have the humility to accept that, while we each have a right to our own convictions, others have a right to theirs too.

I am afraid that the Christmas message of goodwill has usually evaporated by the time Boxing Day is over. This year I hope we will continue to remember the many innocent victims of violence and intolerance and the suffering of their families. Christians are taught to love their neighbours, not just at Christmas, but all the year round.

I hope we will all help each other to have a happy Christmas and, when the New Year comes, resolve to work for tolerance and understanding between all people.

Happy Christmas to you all.

1988

Along with added references to the **Clapham Junction rail crash**, the Lockerbie plane crash **disaster**, and the **Armenian earthquake** that all occurred after the main broadcast was recorded, The Queen reflected on three important anniversaries: the 400th of the **Spanish Armada**, the 300th of the **arrival in Britain** of the future **William III** and **Mary II**, and the **200th of** the founding of Australia.

Sir David Attenborough had to advise Her Majesty that the green dress she was wearing would not work on television because the wallpaper behind her was a similar tone. She reappeared in a more muted hue, observing pointedly that her advisors insisted she wear bright colours in public so that she could be seen easily. The Queen was not amused.

Innumerable newspapers, journals, magazines and books discuss royal appearances and even a single outfit requires sensitive planning by The Queen with her couturier, aides, and always supportive husband.

The Queen and Prince Philip toured Australia in April and May **as part of the bicentenary celebrations.** State visits were to the Netherlands in July and Spain in October.

This Christmas Speech commented on the *'Book of Hours', full of prayers and devotional readings*, with detailed illustrations such as this collage of the Christmas story.

Book of Hours segment from the TV broadcast 1988

Christmas stamp 1988

Recalling anniversaries, The Queen said that *we surely should draw inspiration from one other anniversary - the one we celebrate every year at this time, the birth of Christ.*

There are many grand and splendid pictures in the Royal Collection that illustrate this event, but one which gives me particular pleasure is this precious, almost jewel-like book.

It is a 'Book of Hours', full of prayers and devotional readings. It's in Latin, but it contains the most exquisite illuminations and it is these that speak to us most movingly. The anonymous person who drew the pictures nearly five hundred years ago has included all the familiar elements of the Christmas story which we hear with such pleasure every year.

Here are the angels, bringing the glad tidings to the shepherds, who listen attentively. Down here, where baby Jesus lies in the stall, you can see Mary and Joseph, watching over him, quite unmoved, it seems, by the man playing the bagpipes overhead.

The star over the stable has lit the way for all of us ever since, and there should be no one who feels shut out from that welcoming and guiding light. The legends of Christmas about the ox and the ass suggest that even the animals are not outside that loving care. ...

May the Christmas story encourage you, for it is a message of hope every year, not for a few, but for all.

1989

The Queen read part of her Christmas speech from a podium on the stage at the **Royal Albert Hall**, recorded at a special Save the Children Fund charity carol concert with 2,000 attending. So, for the first time, an audience heard the speech prior to its international broadcast. Her unexpected speech at the event surprised everyone. She also spoke to children at the end of the broadcast. Her message urged children to preserve and protect their world:

You've all seen pictures of the earth taken from space. Unlike all the other planets in the solar system, earth shimmers green and blue in the sunlight and looks a very pleasant place to live.

Major Sir Michael Parker, a veteran of organising royal events, worked with Sir David Attenborough on the broadcast. He reported, "As I escorted The Queen to the stage, no one could work out what on earth was happening. And because they hadn't expected The Queen to speak, no one was ready to memorise what she said. It didn't go in the papers."

During the year The Queen visited Barbados in March for the 350th Anniversary of their parliament and in October she attended the Commonwealth Heads of Government Meeting in Kuala Lumpur, Malaysia.

The surprise Christmas Speech to the children at the charity carol concert encouraged them to be thoughtful and kind as shown in Jesus' story of the Good Samaritan.

Earth from space, NASA

Christmas stamps 1989
Annunciation, Shepherds, Magi

The Queen said that *technical skills are not enough by themselves. They can only come to the rescue of the planet if we also learn to live by the golden rule which Jesus Christ taught us - "love thy neighbour as thyself".*

Many of you will have heard the story of the Good Samaritan, and of how Christ answered the question (from a clever lawyer who was trying to catch him out) "Who is my neighbour?".

Jesus told of the traveller who was mugged and left injured on the roadside where several important people saw him, and passed by without stopping to help.

His neighbour was the man who did stop, cared for him, and made sure he was being well looked after before he resumed his own journey. ...

You children have something to give us which is priceless. You can still look at the world with a sense of wonder and remind us grown-ups that life is wonderful and precious. Often a child's helplessness and vulnerability bring out the best in us.

Part of that 'best in us' could be a particular tenderness towards this earth which we share as human beings, all of us, and, together, as the nations of the world, will leave to our children and our children's children. We must be kind to it for their sake.

In the hope that we will be kind and loving to one another, not just on Christmas Day, but throughout the year, I wish you all a very Happy Christmas. God bless you.

1990

Queen Elizabeth paid tribute to the role of the armed services in the context of imminent war in the **Persian Gulf with the invasion of Kuwait**. The Royal Family and the nation celebrated Queen Elizabeth The Queen Mother turning 90 this year.

The Queen toured New Zealand in February and attended the 14th Commonwealth Games held in Auckland from 24 January to 3 February with 55 nations participating. The Queen's representative, Prince Edward, her youngest son, opened the Games and The Queen and Prince Philip attended for the closing speech by The Queen.

She returned to Canada at the end of June. State visits included Iceland in June and Germany in November.

The Christmas Speech reminded us that *"Christ did not promise the earth to the powerful."*

Queen Victoria and Queen Elizabeth II
Commemorating 150 years of adhesive postage stamps

Christmas stamp 1990

Nowadays there are all too many causes that press their claims with a loud voice and a strong arm rather than with the language of reason. We must not allow ourselves to be too discouraged as we confront them.

Let us remember that Christ did not promise the earth to the powerful. The resolve of those who endure and resist these activities should not be underestimated. ...

I want, therefore, to say thank you today to the men and women who, day in and day out, carry on their daily life in difficult and dangerous circumstances. By just getting on with the job, they are getting the better of those who want to harm our way of life.

Let us think of them this Christmas, wherever they are in the world, and pray that their resolution remains undiminished. It is they and their kind who, by resisting the bully and the tyrant, ensure that we live in the sort of world in which we can celebrate this season safely with our families.

I pray also that we may all be blessed with something of their spirit. Then we would find it easier to solve our disputes in peace and justice, wherever they occur, and that inheritance of the earth which Christ promised, not to the strong, but to the meek, would be that much closer.

A Happy Christmas and God bless you all.

1991

This message reflected on the enormous changes taking place across **Eastern Europe** and **Russia**, which included the **dissolution of the Soviet Union**, the first elections in Russia and the importance of democratic traditions.

The Queen made a one day visit to Northern Ireland on 29 June 1991 and an overnight stop in Kenya on the way to Harare in Zimbabwe for the Commonwealth Heads of Government Meeting in October.

During the official welcome on the White House lawn for The Queen's state visit to the United States in May, the high podium, set for tall President Bush, hid the Queen's face behind microphones. The world's media reported that only the Queen's purple and white striped hat poked up behind the microphones. With typical humour the Queen began her speech the next day to the joint houses of Congress saying, *"I do hope you can see me today from where you are."* The politicians responded with noisy applause.

This year's Christmas Speech referred to the Christian faith's *"message of unselfishness, compassion and tolerance."*

The Queen with President Bush at the White House lawn, 1991

Christmas stamps 1991

This Christmas we can take heart in seeing how, in the former Soviet Union and Eastern Europe, where it has endured years of persecution and hardship, the Christian faith is once again thriving and able to spread its message of unselfishness, compassion and tolerance.

Next February will see the fortieth anniversary of my father's death and of my Accession. Over the years I have tried to follow my father's example and to serve you as best I can.

You have given me, in return, your loyalty and your understanding, and for that I give you my heartfelt thanks. I feel the same obligation to you that I felt in 1952. With your prayers, and your help, and with the love and support of my family, I shall try to serve you in the years to come.

May God bless you and bring you a Happy Christmas.

1992

This Christmas Speech described 1992 as a sombre year. A devastating fire on The Queen and Duke's 45th wedding anniversary, 20 November, destroyed more than 100 rooms in Windsor Castle, the seat of monarchy for a millennium since William the Conqueror. The Queen said, in a speech to Guildhall four days later, *"1992 is not a year on which I shall look back with undiluted pleasure. In the words of one of my more sympathetic correspondents, it has turned out to be an annus horribilis"* – Latin for a horrible year.

The Queen noted in her Guildhall speech: *"A well-meaning Bishop was obviously doing his best when he told Queen Victoria, 'Ma'am, we cannot pray too often, nor too fervently, for the Royal Family.' The Queen's reply was: 'Too fervently, no; too often, yes.' I, like Queen Victoria, have always been a believer in that old maxim 'moderation in all things.'"*

On this 40th Anniversary of her Christmas Speeches, again broadcast from Sandringham, The Queen highlighted the importance of personal fortitude, as shown in the armed services and with aid workers undertaking difficult peacekeeping duties, and in Leonard Cheshire who died that year. *The Sun* published the speech prior to the broadcast, so was required to make a very large donation to charity.

Brief visits included travelling to Australia in February, to Canada in June-July and state visits to France in June and Germany in October.

The Christmas Broadcast reflected on the ways in which *"inspiration can change human behaviour."*

Christmas stamps 1992

Curiously enough, it was a sad event which did as much as anything in 1992 to help me put my own worries into perspective. Just before he died, Leonard Cheshire came to see us with his fellow members of the Order of Merit. ...

One of his Cheshire Homes for people with disabilities is not far from this house. I have visited others all over the Commonwealth and I have seen at first hand the remarkable results of his, and his wife's, determination to put Christ's teaching to practical effect. ...

There is no magic formula that will transform sorrow into happiness, intolerance into compassion or war into peace, but inspiration can change human behaviour.

Those, like Leonard Cheshire, who devote their lives to others, have that inspiration and they know, and we know, where to look for help in finding it. That help can be readily given if we only have the faith to ask.

I and my family, as we approach a new year, will draw strength from this faith in our commitment to your service in the coming years.

I pray that each and every one of you has a happy Christmas and that we can all try to bring that happiness to others. God bless you all.

1993

This broadcast was filmed in the Library at Sandringham. The Queen praised the achievements of volunteers working for peace and for the relief of others. Amid so much bad news there is still the good news.

Again The Queen praised the often unseen and unnoticed work of vast numbers of selfless people helping others and she talked about how the nations can assist others in need. She observed:

We, the peoples of the fifty nations of the Commonwealth - more than a quarter of the world's population - have, as members of one of the largest families, a great responsibility. By working together, we can help the rest of the world become a more humane and happier place.

The royal travels took The Queen to Limassol, Cyprus, for the Commonwealth Heads of Government Meeting in October, where once again those representatives worked together for the betterment of everyone. State visits were to Hungary in May and Belgium in August.

The Christmas Speech gave a beautiful summary of the eternal Good News including, on YouTube, lines from the carol 'O Little Town of Bethlehem'.

Royal Mail commemorative stamps 1993
Bicentenary of Charles Dickens' birth and
150th Anniversary of A Christmas Carol, 1843

Christmas stamps 1993
Peace, Goodwill, Joy

I am always moved by those words in St. John's Gospel which we hear on Christmas Day - "He was in the world, and the world was made by him, and the world knew him not".

We have only to listen to the news to know the truth of that. But the Gospel goes on - "But as many as received him, to them gave he power to become the sons of God".

For all the inhumanity around us, let us be grateful for those who have received him and who go about quietly doing their work and His will without thought of reward or recognition.

They know that there is an eternal truth of much greater significance than our own triumphs and tragedies, and it is embodied by the Child in the Manger. That is their message of hope.

We can all try to reflect that message of hope in our own lives, in our actions and in our prayers. If we do, the reflection may light the way for others and help them to read the message too. ...

I am reminded this year of some lines from a Christmas hymn which many of you will know: "Yet in thy dark streets shineth the everlasting light. The hopes and fears of all the years are met in thee tonight."

I hope you all enjoy your Christmas. I pray, with you, for a happy and peaceful New Year.

1994

Reflecting on past and present peace efforts, Elizabeth spoke about attending the ceremonies marking the 50th anniversary of the **Normandy Landings** in France and her historic first **state visit** to Russia. The state visits this year were to France in May and Russia in October. The broadcast was filmed in The Queen's study at Sandringham.

A corgi found its way into the study during the filming. **Philip Gilbert, a BBC** producer, recalled, "The Queen was speaking to camera absolutely flawlessly when this corgi suddenly walked past me. It started nuzzling The Queen's leg. Without anything showing on camera, she put her hand down and held the dog still, while continuing with the final third of her speech as if nothing had happened."

February and March saw the Royals touring the Caribbean islands of Anguilla, Dominica, Guyana, Belize, Cayman Islands, Jamaica, the Bahamas and Bermuda, and in August they visited Canada at the time of the Commonwealth Games.

The 15th Commonwealth Games were held in Victoria, in British Columbia, Canada, in August, with 63 nations participating. The Games were opened by The Queen's representative Prince Edward and closed by The Queen. It saw South Africa's return after 30 years of the apartheid era and it was the last appearance by Hong Kong before its transfer to China in 1997.

Reflecting on the opportunity to worship with the **Patriarch of Moscow and** his congregation in *"a service in that wonderful cathedral in the heart of the Moscow Kremlin,"* The Queen expressed gratitude that at Christmas *"cathedrals and churches will be full and that the great bells, which greeted us, will be ringing out to celebrate our Saviour's birth."*

Christmas stamps 1994
Toscanni: The Adoration of the Magi

I never thought it would be possible in my lifetime to join with the Patriarch of Moscow and his congregation in a service in that wonderful cathedral in the heart of the Moscow Kremlin.

This Christmas, as we pray for peace at home and abroad - not least in Russia itself - we can also give thanks that such cathedrals and churches will be full and that the great bells, which greeted us, will be ringing out to celebrate our Saviour's birth. ...

Christ taught us to love our enemies and to do good to them that hate us. It is a hard lesson to learn, but this year we have seen shining examples of that generosity of spirit which alone can banish division and prejudice.

... If we resolve to be considerate and to help our neighbours; to make friends with people of different races and religions; and, as our Lord said, to look to our own faults before we criticise others, we will be keeping faith with those who landed in Normandy and fought so doggedly for their belief in freedom, peace and human decency.

1995

In 1995 The Queen and The Queen Mother led national celebrations for the 50th anniversary of the end of World War II. The Queen also paid her first visit to South Africa since 1947, as the guest of President Nelson Mandela. Royal visits included South Africa in March and New Zealand for the Commonwealth Heads of Government Meeting in October-November.

As well as the commemorations for the end of the war, there were encouraging signs that peace was finally coming to Northern Ireland. The visit to South Africa showed how disputes and hatred could be overcome if stood up for change. This was the theme in her Christmas address.

The Queen's Christmas Broadcast reflected on the role of ordinary men and women in bringing peace as with the example of a nun helping huge numbers of needy people in South Africa:

It is the ordinary men and women who, so often, have done more than anyone else to bring peace to troubled lands. ...

During my visit to South Africa last March, I was able to see, in a township, how the energy and inspiration of one person could benefit thousands of others. And that one person would lay no claim to be anything other than ordinary - whatever you or I might think of her!

The Queen, The Queen Mother, and Princess Margaret
50th Anniversary, end of World War II

Christmas stamp 1995

I have of course used the Christmas story before in this context. But I cannot think of any Christmas of my reign when the message of the angels has been more apt.

Think, for instance, of all the children round the world suffering from the effects of war and the unscrupulous use of power. Some of them are growing up in countries of the Commonwealth, an organisation which is proud of its devotion to the principle of good government. ...

"Blessed be the peacemakers," Christ said, "for they shall be called the children of God." It is especially to those of you, often peacemakers without knowing it, who are fearful of a troubled and uncertain future, that I bid a Happy Christmas.

It is your good sense and good will which have achieved so much. It must not and will not go to waste. May there be still happier Christmases to come, for you and your children. You deserve the best of them.

Happy Christmas and God bless you all.

1996

The Queen spoke of her trips to **Poland**, the **Czech Republic**, and **Thailand**, as well as the visit to the United Kingdom by South African President Nelson Mandela. The theme of this message was hope for the future.

In March 1996, Royal Family members travelled to Dunblane, Scotland, to visit the families of 15 schoolchildren and their teacher who had been shot in a massacre. The Scottish press recorded The Queen weeping openly and turning to Princess Anne for support as she spoke to the parents of the victims.

Then, also in March The Queen and Prince Philip made state visits to Poland and the Czech Republic. Their state visit to Thailand was in October.

The Queen commented on Nelson Mandela, President of the new South Africa:

And I shall never forget the State Visit of President Mandela. The most gracious of men has shown us all how to accept the facts of the past without bitterness, how to see new opportunities as more important than old disputes and how to look forward with courage and optimism.

His example is a continuing inspiration to the whole Commonwealth and to all those everywhere who work for peace and reconciliation.

President Nelson Mandela with The Queen

Christmas stamps 1996

Christmas is the celebration of the birth of the founder of the Christian faith, an event which took place almost 2000 years ago; every year, at this time, we are asked to look back at that extraordinary story and remind ourselves of the message which inspired Christ's followers then, and which is just as relevant today.

At Christmas I enjoy looking back on some of the events of the year. Many have their roots in history but still have a real point for us today. I recall, especially, a dazzling spring day in Norwich when I attended the Maundy Service, the Cathedral providing a spectacular setting.

The lovely service is always a reminder of Christ's words to his disciples: "Love one another; as I have loved you". It sounds so simple yet it proves so hard to obey. ...

If only we can live up to the example of the child who was born at Christmas with a love that came to embrace the whole world. If only we can let him recapture for us that time when we faced the future with childhood's unbounded faith.

Armed with that faith, the New Year, with all its challenges and chances, should hold no terrors for us, and we should be able to embark upon it undaunted.

My family joins me in wishing each one of you a very Happy Christmas.

1997

This first Christmas message produced by **Independent Television News**, as well as being the first to be published on the Internet, began with contrasting pictures of **Westminster Abbey**, for the **funeral** of **Diana, Princess of Wales**, and for the celebration of The Queen and Prince Philip's golden wedding anniversary. The Queen reflected:

At the Christian heart of this United Kingdom stands Westminster Abbey, and it was right that it provided the setting for two events this year – one of them almost unbearably sad, and one, for Prince Philip and me, tremendously happy.

The Queen spoke about her trips to Canada, to India and **Pakistan on the 50 anniversary of their independence in 1947**, and of the **return of Hong Kong to China which laid the old Empire to rest. This year in Edinburgh she met with the Heads of the Commonwealth.**

In August, Her Majesty sailed for two weeks with 16 of her family on the royal yacht Britannia for the last of the Western Isles cruises. HMY Britannia was decommissioned in December. The Royal Family cared for and protected the young Princes William and Harry at Balmoral after the boys' mother died in the Paris car crash on Saturday, 31 August.

They returned to London on 5 September, the eve of Diana's funeral. At Buckingham Palace they mingled with the mourning crowd at the flower-decked railings. Eleven-year-old Katie Jones handed The Queen five red roses. "Would you like me to place them for you?" The Queen asked. "No, they're for you, Ma'am" Katie replied. "Are you sure?" "Yes, I think you deserve them. I think you've done the right thing staying with your grandsons. I think if my mum had just died I'd want my grandmother with me." The crowd began to clap.

The restoration of Windsor Castle was completed in November, five years after fire damaged over 100 rooms. For that reason The Queen's Christmas Broadcast this year came from the White Drawing Room at Windsor Castle.

The Speech noted that *"St Paul spoke of the first Christmas as the kindness of God dawning upon the world"* and how *"Christmas reassures us that God is with us today."*

Christmas stamps 1997

For most of us this is a happy family day. But I am well aware that there are many of you who are alone, bereaved, or suffering. My heart goes out to you, and I pray that we, the more fortunate ones, can unite to lend a helping hand whenever it is needed, and not 'pass by on the other side'.

St Paul spoke of the first Christmas as the kindness of God dawning upon the world. The world needs that kindness now more than ever - the kindness and consideration for others that disarms malice and allows us to get on with one another with respect and affection.

Christmas reassures us that God is with us today. But, as I have discovered afresh for myself this year, he is always present in the kindness shown by our neighbours and the love of our friends and family.

God bless you all and Happy Christmas.

1998

This year's message focused on lessons that could be learnt by different generations from each other, and the broadcast included film of **Queen Elizabeth The Queen Mother**. It also showed The Queen at **Ypres** and in **Paris**, and the reception for the Prince of Wales' 50th birthday.

The 16th Commonwealth Games, in Kuala Lumpur, Malaysia in September introduced the team sports of rugby sevens, netball, hockey and cricket. A record 70 nations participated in these first Commonwealth Games held in Asia. Again The Queen officially closed the Games.

There was a state visit early in November to Belgium. Royal tours in Africa in November were to Ghana, to South Africa for the Commonwealth Heads meetings, and to Mozambique.

The Broadcast this year emphasized that *"Christmas is a time for reflection and renewal."*

Queen Elizabeth The Queen Mother
From the Christmas Broadcast 1998

Christmas stamp 1998

Christmas is a time for reflection and renewal. For Christians the year's end has a special and familiar significance, but all faiths have their calendars, their sign-posts, which ask us to pause from time to time and think further than the hectic daily round. We do that as individuals, with our families, and as members of our local communities. ...

My work, and the work of my family, takes us every week into that quiet sort of 'public life', where millions of people give their time, unpaid and usually unsung, to the community, and indeed to those most at risk of exclusion from it. ...

It is they that help define our sense of duty. It is they that can make us strong as individuals, and keep the nation's heartbeat strong and steady too. Christmas is a good time for us to recognise all that they do for us and to say a heartfelt thank you to each and every one of them.

Happy Christmas to you all.

1999

The Queen's Speech talked about looking forward to the start of a new century and a new millennium, as well as learning from the lessons of history. The broadcast, filmed in the White Drawing Room of Windsor Castle, showed footage of a reception at **the Palace of Holyroodhouse in Edinburgh** for young achievers, and a reception at Buckingham Palace for members of the emergency services.

Prince Edward, youngest son of The Queen and Prince Philip, married **Sophie Rhys-Jones on 19 June in St George's Chapel, Windsor.**

A state visit to South Korea in April was followed in November with a return to Durban, South Africa, for the Commonwealth Heads meeting.

This Christmas Broadcast noted the importance of looking forward as well as looking back:

This December we are looking back not just on one year, but on a hundred years and a thousand years.

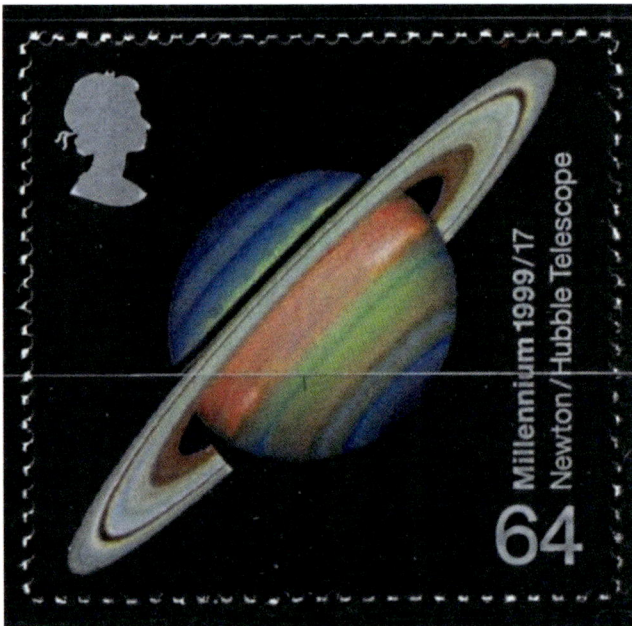

Royal Mail tribute to Isaac Newton,
Hubble Space Telescope photo of Saturn.

Christmas stamps 1999

A very Happy Christmas to you all. Listening to the choir from St. George's Chapel, Windsor, reminds me that this season of carols and Christmas trees is a time to take stock; a time to reflect on the events of the past year and to make resolutions for the new year ahead. ...

The future is not only about new gadgets, modern technology or the latest fashion, important as these may be. At the centre of our lives - today and tomorrow - must be the message of caring for others, the message at the heart of Christianity and of all the great religions.

This message - love thy neighbour as thyself - may be for Christians 2,000 years old. But it is as relevant today as it ever was. I believe it gives us the guidance and the reassurance we need as we step over the threshold into the twenty-first century.

And I for one am looking forward to this new Millennium.

May I wish you all a Merry Christmas and, in this year of all years, a very Happy New Year.

2000

The Queen used her Christmas Broadcast to reflect on the true start of the new millennium and the role of faith in communities. The broadcast included film of this year's visit to Australia.

In March, The Queen and Prince Philip visited Australia, which had voted in a recent referendum to keep Her Majesty as their Queen and Head of State in "this rugged, honest, creative land".

Over 40,000 people gathered outside Buckingham Palace to see the balcony appearance of The Queen, Princess Margaret and The Queen Mother to celebrate The Queen Mother's 100th birthday on the 4 August.

The Queen made a state visit with her husband to Italy and the Vatican City in October. The Italians liked her sense of style, and she was praised by the critical fashion writers as "one of the most elegant women in the world".

The Queen's millennium speech reflected on the millennium's significance.

Christmas is the traditional, if not the actual, birthday of a man who was destined to change the course of our history. And today we are celebrating the fact that Jesus Christ was born two thousand years ago; this is the true Millennium anniversary.

The simple facts of Jesus' life give us little clue as to the influence he was to have on the world. As a boy he learnt his father's trade as a carpenter. He then became a preacher, recruiting twelve supporters to help him.

But his ministry only lasted a few years and he himself never wrote anything down. In his early thirties he was arrested, tortured and crucified with two criminals. His death might have been the end of the story, but then came the resurrection and with it the foundation of the Christian faith.

Even in our very material age the impact of Christ's life is all around us. If you want to see an expression of Christian faith you have only to look at our awe-inspiring cathedrals and abbeys, listen to their music, or look at their stained glass windows, their books and their pictures.

Christmas stamps 2000

But the true measure of Christ's influence is not only in the lives of the saints but also in the good works quietly done by millions of men and women day in and day out throughout the centuries.

Many will have been inspired by Jesus' simple but powerful teaching: love God and love thy neighbour as thyself - in other words, treat others as you would like them to treat you. His great emphasis was to give spirituality a practical purpose. ...

To many of us our beliefs are of fundamental importance. For me the teachings of Christ and my own personal accountability before God provide a framework in which I try to lead my life. I, like so many of you, have drawn great comfort in difficult times from Christ's words and example.

I believe that the Christian message, in the words of a familiar blessing, remains profoundly important to us all:

"Go forth into the world in peace,
be of good courage,
hold fast that which is good,
render to no man evil for evil,
strengthen the faint-hearted,
support the weak,
help the afflicted,
honour all men."

It is a simple message of compassion... and yet as powerful as ever today, two thousand years after Christ's birth.

2001

2001 saw large-scale terrorist attacks on 11 September (9/11) on the World Trade Centre in New York and the Pentagon in Washington, killing around 3,000 people and injuring 6,000 others. More disasters included the outbreak of foot-and-mouth disease in the United Kingdom's farming community, and famine in Sudan. The Queen's Christmas Broadcast this year told how communities can work together to respond to problems and disasters.

The broadcast showed the occasion when on 13 September the **American national anthem** was played at the **changing of the guard at Buckingham Palace**. For the first time, The Queen allowed her troops to play The Star Spangled Banner during the ceremony in tribute to the many who died.

There was a state visit to Norway in May.

This year was the centenary of the Federation of the Commonwealth of Australia, proclaimed on 1 January 1901. In 1950, Australia Post issued stamps depicting **Gwoya Jungarai (c. 1895 – 28 March 1965)**, a Walpiri-Anmatyerre man of the Northern Territory, nicknamed One Pound Jimmy, the first Aborigine featured on an Australian postage stamp. It was Australia's first stamp depicting a living person other than British Royalty.

The Queen's message emphasized the importance of faith when finding strength in troubled times, and paid tribute to those who work for others in the community. Her Christmas Speech told how *"Christ's birth in Bethlehem so long ago remains a powerful symbol of hope for a better future."*

Christmas stamp 2001

It is to the Church that we turn to give meaning to these moments of intense human experience through prayer, symbol and ceremony.

In these circumstances so many of us, whatever our religion, need our faith more than ever to sustain and guide us. Every one of us needs to believe in the value of all that is good and honest; we need to let this belief drive and influence our actions. ...

This is an important lesson for us all during this festive season. For Christmas marks a moment to pause, to reflect and believe in the possibilities of rebirth and renewal.

Christ's birth in Bethlehem so long ago remains a powerful symbol of hope for a better future. After all the tribulations of this year, this is surely more relevant than ever.

As we come together amongst family and friends and look forward to the coming year, I hope that in the months to come we shall be able to find ways of strengthening our own communities as a sure support and comfort to us all - whatever may lie ahead.

May I, in this my fiftieth Christmas message to you, once again wish every one of you a very happy Christmas.

2002

Filmed in the White Drawing Room of Buckingham Palace with photographs of her parents and Princess Margaret by her side, The Queen recalled the joyful celebration of her **Golden Jubilee.** She spoke of the twin pillars of the message of hope in the Christian gospel and the support of the public.

In this 50th anniversary of The Queen's Christmas Broadcast, also the 70th anniversary of the first Christmas Broadcast by George V, The Queen spoke about the deaths of her sister, **Princess Margaret in February**, and her mother, **Queen Elizabeth The Queen Mother** in March, and the comfort she received from her faith and the tributes of others.

The Queen Mother at 100 in 2000 with The Queen and Princess Margaret

The 17th Commonwealth Games were held in Manchester, England, from 25 July to 4 August with a record 72 nations participating. For the first time The Queen officially opened and closed the Games as part of her Golden Jubilee.

Royal visits included Jamaica and New Zealand in February and the Commonwealth Heads meeting in Coolum, Australia, in March.

Her Majesty drew strength from *"the message of hope in the Christian gospel".*

Christmas stamps 2002

Golden Jubilee Australian commemorative stamps

Anniversaries are important events in all our lives. Christmas is the anniversary of the birth of Christ over two thousand years ago, but it is much more than that. It is the celebration of the birth of an idea and an ideal. ...

I know just how much I rely on my own faith to guide me through the good times and the bad. Each day is a new beginning, I know that the only way to live my life is to try to do what is right, to take the long view, to give of my best in all that the day brings, and to put my trust in God.

Like others of you who draw inspiration from your own faith, I draw strength from the message of hope in the Christian gospel.

Fortified by this and the support you have given throughout the last twelve months which has meant so much to me, I look forward to the New Year, to facing the challenges and opportunities that lie ahead, and to continuing to serve you to the very best of my ability each and every day.

A Happy Christmas to you all.

2003

The opening of this broadcast was recorded at the **Household Calvary Barracks** in Windsor. The Queen referred to the many members of Commonwealth armed forces on foreign deployments and paid tribute to the work they did to preserve peace.

The Queen visited Abuja, Nigeria, for the Commonwealth Heads of Government Meetings in December.

Around 10 million in the United Kingdom and millions more worldwide listened. The Speech emphasized the importance of teamwork and voluntary work as demonstrated by those receiving the new **Queen's Golden Jubilee Award for Voluntary Service in the Community.**

Concerning service, the Queen quoted the famous prayer of **Saint Ignatius Loyola (1491-1556)**. That prayer reminds us of the similar famous prayer of St. Francis of Assisi (1182-1226):

Lord make me an instrument of your peace
Where there is hatred let me sow love
Where there is injury, pardon
Where there is doubt, faith
Where there is despair, hope
Where there is darkness, light
And where there is sadness, joy.

O divine master grant that I may
not so much seek to be consoled as to console
to be understood as to understand
to be loved as to love.
For it is in giving that we receive
it is in pardoning that we are pardoned
And it's in dying that we are born to eternal life.
Amen

Christmas stamps 2003

The Founder of the Christian Faith himself chose twelve disciples to help him in his ministry.

In this country and throughout the Commonwealth there are groups of people who are giving their time generously to make a difference to the lives of others.

As we think of them, and of our Servicemen and women far from home at this Christmas time, I hope we all, whatever our faith, can draw inspiration from the words of the familiar prayer:

"Teach us good Lord
To serve thee as thou deservest;
To give, and not to count the cost;
To fight, and not to heed the wounds;
To toil, and not to seek for rest;
To labour, and not to ask for any reward;
Save that of knowing that we do thy will."

It is this knowledge which will help us all to enjoy the Festival of Christmas.

A happy Christmas to you all.

2004

This broadcast showed The Queen handing out presents to her own family, and had coverage of The Queen and Prince Philip visiting a Sikh gurudwara, and Prince Charles visiting a **Muslim** school in east London. The theme of this message was cultural and religious diversity and the benefits of tolerance. The Queen also sent a separate radio Christmas message to troops, which was broadcasted by the **British Forces Broadcasting Service.**

There were state visits to France in April and Germany in November.

On Boxing Day a 9.2 magnitude earthquake followed by a tsunami devastated parts of Southeast Asia. Five of the seven countries most severely affected were Commonwealth members.

Focusing on tolerance and respect, the Christmas Speech this year gave the example of Jesus' *"timeless story of a victim of a mugging who was ignored by his own countrymen but helped by a foreigner - and a despised foreigner at that."*

Christmas stamp 2004

Christmas stamps 2004

Religion and culture are much in the news these days, usually as sources of difference and conflict, rather than for bringing people together. But the irony is that every religion has something to say about tolerance and respecting others.

For me as a Christian one of the most important of these teachings is contained in the parable of the Good Samaritan, when Jesus answers the question "who is my neighbour".

It is a timeless story of a victim of a mugging who was ignored by his own countrymen but helped by a foreigner - and a despised foreigner at that.

The implication drawn by Jesus is clear. Everyone is our neighbour, no matter what race, creed or colour. The need to look after a fellow human being is far more important than any cultural or religious differences. ...

A Happy Christmas to you all.

2005

This year The Queen reflected on tragedies such as the Boxing Day 2004 Indian Ocean tsunami, Hurricane Katrina and the floods in New Orleans, the earthquake in Kashmir which killed over 70,000 people and left millions homeless, and the July bombings in London killing underground commuters. Footage showed ordinary people helping the suffering in practical and financial ways in the remarkable humanitarian responses from people of all faiths.

On 9 April 2005, Prince Charles married Camilla Parker Bowles. Although The Queen did not attend the wedding due to her constitutional position, she gave them a warm endorsement in her speech later that day.

Royal visits were made to Canada in May and to Malta in November for the Commonwealth Heads of Government Meeting.

The Broadcast reminded us that *"Christmas is the time to remember the birth of the one we call 'the Prince of Peace' and our source of 'light and life' in both good times and bad."*

Royal Mail commemorative stamps
Prince Charles and Mrs Camilla Parker Bowles

Christmas stamps 2005

This Christmas my thoughts are especially with those everywhere who are grieving the loss of loved ones during what for so many has been such a terrible year. ...

There may be an instinct in all of us to help those in distress, but in many cases I believe this has been inspired by religious faith. Christianity is not the only religion to teach its followers to help others and to treat your neighbour as you would want to be treated yourself.

It has been clear that in the course of this year relief workers and financial support have come from members of every faith and from every corner of the world. ...

This last year has reminded us that this world is not always an easy or a safe place to live in, but it is the only place we have. I believe also that it has shown us all how our faith - whatever our religion - can inspire us to work together in friendship and peace for the sake of our own and future generations.

For Christians this festival of Christmas is the time to remember the birth of the one we call "the Prince of Peace" and our source of "light and life" in both good times and bad. It is not always easy to accept his teaching, but I have no doubt that the New Year will be all the better if we do but try.

I hope you will all have a very happy Christmas this year and that you go into the New Year with renewed hope and confidence.

2006

This year marked The Queen's 80th birthday. Her Christmas Broadcast focused on greater understanding between faiths and generations. The broadcast, available for the first time for download as a podcast, was filmed in Southwark Cathedral in London where Her Majesty met schoolchildren working on a Nativity collage.

The 18th Commonwealth Games, held in Melbourne, Australia between 15 and 26 March with 71 nations competing, were officially opened by The Queen and closed by her son Prince Edward. State visits took them to Lithuania, Latvia and Estonia in October.

Other royal events this year included the visit to Australia in March for the 18th Commonwealth Games and also to Singapore in March. This year Prince Charles' sons, The Queen's grandsons, both graduated from the Royal Military Academy Sandhurst, Prince Harry on 12 April and Prince William on 15 December, with smiles shared at the Sovereign's Parade.

The Christmas Speech observed that *"for Christians, Christmas marks the birth of our Saviour, but it is also a wonderful occasion to bring the generations together in a shared festival of peace, tolerance and goodwill."*

Princes Harry and William at the Sovereign's Parades, 2006

Christmas stamps 2006

I have lived long enough to know that things never remain quite the same for very long. One of the things that has not changed all that much for me is the celebration of Christmas. It remains a time when I try to put aside the anxieties of the moment and remember that Christ was born to bring peace and tolerance to a troubled world.

The birth of Jesus naturally turns our thoughts to all new-born children and what the future holds for them. The birth of a baby brings great happiness - but then the business of growing up begins. It is a process that starts within the protection and care of parents and other members of the family - including the older generation. As with any team, there is strength in combination: what grandparent has not wished for the best possible upbringing for their grandchildren or felt an enormous sense of pride at their achievements? ...

For Christians, Christmas marks the birth of our Saviour, but it is also a wonderful occasion to bring the generations together in a shared festival of peace, tolerance and goodwill.

I wish you all a very happy Christmas together.

2007

The 2007 message began with a replay of the introductory remarks from the 1957 Christmas message, the first shown on television, and The Queen standing beside that first televised broadcast. This year was the sovereign's Diamond Wedding with the photos on the next page taken at Malta, 60 years apart, where Prince Philip had served as an officer in the Royal Navy.

Royal visits included returning to Malta on 20 November, 60 years after the honeymoon there, and meeting with Commonwealth Heads of Government in Kampala, Uganda, in November. State visits were to the Netherlands in February, the United States in May and Belgium in July.

The theme on the family included the need to care for the vulnerable. The broadcast included footage of the **Royal Marines** in **Afghanistan** as well as a military memorial. The message ended with a black and white clip of **"God Save The Queen"** from the original television broadcast in 1957 and an image of the **British royal standard**.

Quoting from The Bidding Prayer in A Service of Lessons and Carols in the *Handbook of the Christian Year*, Her Majesty concluded her speech with this reminder: ***A familiar introduction to an annual Christmas Carol Service contains the words: "Because this would most rejoice his heart, let us remember, in his name, the poor and the helpless, the cold, the hungry, and the oppressed; the sick and those who mourn, the lonely and the unloved."*** That quotation from the Bidding Prayer points to Jesus' concern for the poor and helpless, the theme for this year's Christmas message.

Christmas stamp 2007
50 Years of Christmas Stamps

Diamond Wedding Anniversary

Now today, of course, marks the birth of Jesus Christ. Among other things, it is a reminder that it is the story of a family; but of a family in very distressed circumstances. Mary and Joseph found no room at the inn; they had to make do in a stable, and the new-born Jesus had to be laid in a manger. This was a family which had been shut out.

Perhaps it was because of this early experience that, throughout his ministry, Jesus of Nazareth reached out and made friends with people whom others ignored or despised. It was in this way that he proclaimed his belief that, in the end, we are all brothers and sisters in one human family.

The Christmas story also draws attention to all those people who are on the edge of society - people who feel cut off and disadvantaged; people who, for one reason or another, are not able to enjoy the full benefits of living in a civilised and law-abiding community. For these people the modern world can seem a distant and hostile place.

It is all too easy to 'turn a blind eye', 'to pass by on the other side', and leave it to experts and professionals. All the great religious teachings of the world press home the message that everyone has a responsibility to care for the vulnerable.

2008

This Christmas Speech was the first message broadcast in **high-definition as well as in standard definition television and on radio.** It was filmed in the Music Room at Buckingham Palace where Prince Charles, the Prince of Wales had been baptised 60 years previously.

The Queen acknowledged that concerns about the **2008 economic downturn** as well as violence around the world made that year's Christmas *"a more sombre occasion for many"* and she called on people to show courage and not to accept defeat but to struggle for a better future.

She reflected on the 60th birthday of the **Prince of Wales** and mentioned his charitable work and the service of his sons, and paid tribute to those who lead charitable lives in the service of others.

State visits were made to Turkey in May and to Slovenia and Slovakia in October.

This year's Broadcast affirmed that *"two thousand years after the birth of Jesus, so many of us are able to draw inspiration from his life and message, and to find in him a source of strength and courage."*

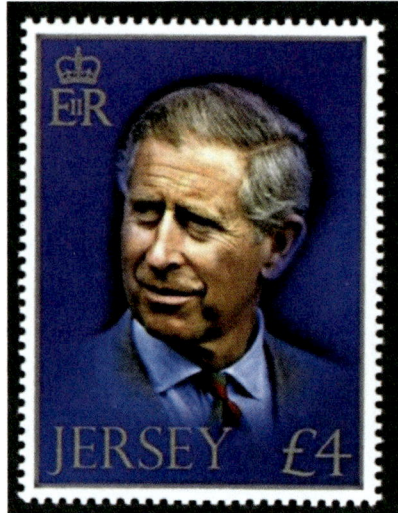

Prince Charles at 60

Christmas stamps 2008

At Christmas, we feel very fortunate to have our family around us. But for many of you, this Christmas will mean separation from loved ones and perhaps reflection on the memories of those no longer with us.

I hope that, like me, you will be comforted by the example of Jesus of Nazareth who, often in circumstances of great adversity, managed to live an outgoing, unselfish and sacrificial life. Countless millions of people around the world continue to celebrate his birthday at Christmas, inspired by his teaching. He makes it clear that genuine human happiness and satisfaction lie more in giving than receiving; more in serving than in being served.

We can surely be grateful that, two thousand years after the birth of Jesus, so many of us are able to draw inspiration from his life and message, and to find in him a source of strength and courage. I hope that the Christmas message will encourage and sustain you too, now and in the coming year.

I wish you all a very happy Christmas.

2009

The Queen reflected on the important role of Commonwealth armed forces serving in Afghanistan, involving well over 13,000 soldiers from the United Kingdom, Canada, Australia, New Zealand and Singapore.

This year marked 60 years since the Commonwealth of Nations was formed in 1949, and The Queen noted how the personal and living bond she has had with leaders and people *"has always been more important in promoting our unity than symbolism alone."*

She spoke about the significance of new technologies, especially for young people and the future and how the Commonwealth can strengthen the common bond that transcends politics, religion, race and economic circumstances.

The Queen visited Bermuda, Trinidad and Tobago in November when attending the Commonwealth Heads of Government Meeting at Port of Spain, Trinidad.

The Christmas Speech recognized that *"Christmas is a time for celebration and family reunions; but it is also a time to reflect on what confronts those less fortunate than ourselves."*

Trinidad & Tobago Commemorative Stamps

Christmas stamps 2009

We know that Christmas is a time for celebration and family reunions; but it is also a time to reflect on what confronts those less fortunate than ourselves, at home and throughout the world.

Christians are taught to love their neighbours, having compassion and concern, and being ready to undertake charity and voluntary work to ease the burden of deprivation and disadvantage. We may ourselves be confronted by a bewildering array of difficulties and challenges, but we must never cease to work for a better future for ourselves and for others.

I wish you all, wherever you may be, a very happy Christmas.

2010

This Christmas message, filmed in **Hampton Court Palace**, focused on the importance of the King James Bible (400 years old in 2011) as a unifying force, and of sport doing so also. The Queen referred to **the Winter Paralympics, held in Canada in March, and to the role of sport** in building communities and creating harmony. The broadcast included footage of **Prince William** and **Prince Harry** playing football with orphans in **Lesotho in Africa.**

The Royals visited Canada, 28 June to 6 July, and in October Prince Charles opened the 19th Commonwealth Games in Delhi, India, with the President of India, with 71 teams competing. They had state visits to the United Arab Emirates and Oman in November.

The title page to the 1611 first edition of the Authorized Version of the Bible shows the Apostles Peter and Paul seated centrally above the central text, which is flanked by Moses and Aaron. In the four corners sit Matthew, Mark, Luke and John, authors of the four gospels, with their symbolic animals. The rest of the Apostles (with Judas facing away) stand around Peter and Paul. At the very top is the Tetragrammaton "יְהֹוָה" [YHWH] in Hebrew diacritics.

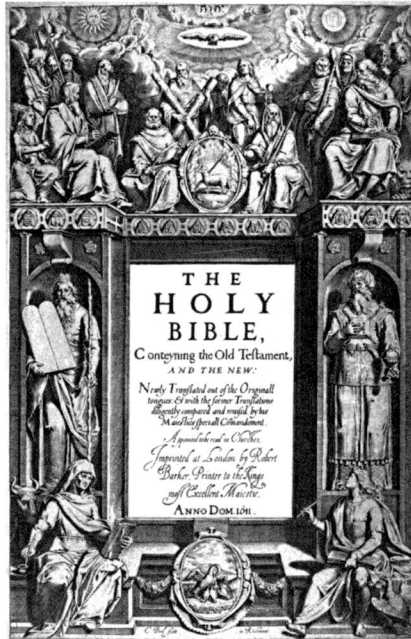

Christmas stamps 2010

Over four hundred years ago, King James the Sixth of Scotland inherited the throne of England at a time when the Christian Church was deeply divided. Here at Hampton Court in 1604, he convened a conference of churchmen of all shades of opinion to discuss the future of Christianity in this country. The King agreed to commission a new translation of the Bible that was acceptable to all parties. This was to become the King James or Authorized Bible, which next year will be exactly four centuries old.

Acknowledged as a masterpiece of English prose and the most vivid translation of the scriptures, the glorious language of this Bible has survived the turbulence of history and given many of us the most widely-recognised and beautiful descriptions of the birth of Jesus Christ which we celebrate today. ...

People are capable of belonging to many communities, including a religious faith. King James may not have anticipated quite how important sport and games were to become in promoting harmony and common interests. But from the scriptures in the Bible which bears his name, we know that nothing is more satisfying than the feeling of belonging to a group who are dedicated to helping each other:

'Therefore all things whatsoever ye would that men should to do to you, do ye even so to them'. [Matthew 7:12]

2011

Unity and hope amid adversity and the importance of family and of the Commonwealth, a family of 53 nations, were themes in this year's broadcast. The message was recorded on 9 December, prior to the Duke of Edinburgh's hospitalisation for emergency heart surgery, and was the first Christmas message produced by **Sky News**.

Prince Philip accompanied The Queen on the historic **state visit to the Republic of Ireland from 17 May to 20 May, the first visit by a reigning British monarch to the Republic of Ireland in a century, since the 1911 tour by King George V.**

Buckingham Palace hosted the state visit of President Barack and Michelle Obama on 24-25 May. When the President asked everyone to stand for the royal toast, the band mistook that as a signal to play the National Anthem, an unusual musical interruption to the royal toast.

The year included a return visit by The Queen and Prince Philip to Australia in October, including meeting Commonwealth Heads of Government in Perth during CHOGM (October 28-30). This visit, her 16th to Australia, was called the Farewell Tour as it was likely to be her last there. She described the Commonwealth as a family of nations "*with a common bond, shared beliefs, mutual values and goals.*"

The Queen spoke about Prince William's visit to New Zealand and Australia in the aftermath of earthquakes, cyclones and floods, and the visit of the Prince of Wales to a Welsh mining community struck by tragedy. Both men saw resilient communities rebuilding and helping to support each other.

The weddings of two of The Queen's grandchildren, **Prince William to Catherine Middleton**, and **Zara Phillips** to Mike Tindall, were "*each in their own way a celebration of the God-given love that binds a family together.*"

The Queen's prayer in this Broadcast was that "*we might all find room in our lives for the message of the angels and for the love of God through Christ our Lord.*"

Christmas stamps 2011

Finding hope in adversity is one of the themes of Christmas. Jesus was born into a world full of fear. The angels came to frightened shepherds with hope in their voices: 'Fear not', they urged, 'we bring you tidings of great joy, which shall be to all people. For unto you is born this day in the City of David a Saviour who is Christ the Lord.'

Although we are capable of great acts of kindness, history teaches us that we sometimes need saving from ourselves - from our recklessness or our greed.

God sent into the world a unique person - neither a philosopher nor a general, important though they are, but a Saviour, with the power to forgive. Forgiveness lies at the heart of the Christian faith. It can heal broken families, it can restore friendships and it can reconcile divided communities. It is in forgiveness that we feel the power of God's love.

In the last verse of this beautiful carol, O Little Town of Bethlehem, there's a prayer:
O Holy Child of Bethlehem,
Descend to us we pray.
Cast out our sin
And enter in.
Be born in us today.

It is my prayer that on this Christmas day we might all find room in our lives for the message of the angels and for the love of God through Christ our Lord.

2012

Broadcast for the first time in **3D**, this message in her Diamond Jubilee year was the 60th Queen's Christmas Speech and the 80th anniversary of the Christmas messages. This **year it focused on service, achievement and the spirit of togetherness.**

Recalling the duty which passed to her 60 years ago, The Queen praised the strength of friendship and fellowship of everyone involved in the many celebrations, especially the Diamond Jubilee tribute on the River Thames, in the rain and mist, involving 1,000 craft from across the Commonwealth. The memorable Jubilee service in Westminster Abbey in June was followed two weeks later with her horse Estimate winning the Gold Cup at Royal Ascot.

The Queen's Speech acknowledged the sacrificial service of those in the armed forces, emergency services and hospitals whose duty takes them away from family and friends. London hosted the Olympic and Paralympic Games that year and the sovereign praised those involved including the army of volunteers devoted to keeping others safe, supported and comforted. The Queen, with corgis, featured in the Olympic Games opening ceremony film with Daniel Craig playing James Bond.

King George VI, her father, introduced young Elizabeth to Pembroke Welsh corgis when he brought home Dookie in 1933, soon followed by Jane and by her puppies Crackers and Carol (so named because they were born on Christmas Eve). At 18 Princess Elizabeth was given her own corgi, Susan, from whom all hers are descended. Susan's grave in 1959 at Sandringham bears the simple inscription, 'The faithful companion of The Queen'. Many of her other dogs buried there have the same affectionate epitaph.

Her Majesty's prayer in this message is that Jesus' "*example and teaching will continue to bring people together to give the best of themselves in the service of others.*"

Christmas stamps 2012

First Christmas Broadcast in 3D

At Christmas I am always struck by how the spirit of togetherness lies also at the heart of the Christmas story. A young mother and a dutiful father with their baby were joined by poor shepherds and visitors from afar. They came with their gifts to worship the Christ child. From that day on he has inspired people to commit themselves to the best interests of others.

This is the time of year when we remember that God sent his only son 'to serve, not to be served'. He restored love and service to the centre of our lives in the person of Jesus Christ.

It is my prayer this Christmas Day that his example and teaching will continue to bring people together to give the best of themselves in the service of others.

The carol, In The Bleak Midwinter, ends by asking a question of all of us who know the Christmas story, of how God gave himself to us in humble service: 'What can I give him, poor as I am? If I were a shepherd, I would bring a lamb; if I were a wise man, I would do my part'. The carol gives the answer 'Yet what I can I give him - give my heart'.

I wish you all a very happy Christmas.

2013

The 60th anniversary of the Coronation in 1953 gave opportunity for reflection on the changes since then and the things remaining constant such as family, friendship and good neighbourliness.

The speech considered the importance of a balance between action and reflection:

Be it through contemplation, prayer, or even keeping a diary, many have found the practice of quiet personal reflection surprisingly rewarding, even discovering greater spiritual depth to their lives.

The Queen reflected on Christmas as a time when family and friends reminisce and remember those away from home.

She spoke about the significance of the upcoming 2014 Commonwealth Games in Glasgow and the recent Commonwealth Heads of Government Meeting in Colombo, Sri Lanka (15-17 November) with a clip of the Prince of Wales' speech to Commonwealth leaders included in the broadcast.

Her reflections included reference to the birth and christening of her great-grandchild, Prince George, and the Royal Family's traditional photograph now bringing together four generations.

This Speech tells how *"reflection, meditation and prayer help us to renew ourselves in God's love and that the Christmas message shows us that this love is for everyone. There is no one beyond its reach."*

Prince George commemorative stamp

Christmas stamps 2013

In the year ahead, I hope you will have time to pause for moments of quiet reflection. ...

For Christians, as for all people of faith, reflection, meditation and prayer help us to renew ourselves in God's love, as we strive daily to become better people. The Christmas message shows us that this love is for everyone. There is no one beyond its reach.

On the first Christmas, in the fields above Bethlehem, as they sat in the cold of night watching their resting sheep, the local shepherds must have had no shortage of time for reflection. Suddenly all this was to change. These humble shepherds were the first to hear and ponder the wondrous news of the birth of Christ – the first noel – the joy of which we celebrate today.

2014

The Queen spoke about reconciliation, the centenary of the outbreak of World War I and the ceramic poppy memorial at the Tower of London, the 70 countries involved in the Commonwealth Games in Glasgow followed by the first Invictus Games in London, her historic visit to Belfast, the Northern Ireland peace process, and the referendum in Scotland. She praised *"the selflessness of aid workers and medical volunteers who have gone abroad to help victims of conflict or of diseases like Ebola, often at great personal risk."*

The Queen officially opened the 20th Commonwealth Games, held 23 July to 3 August in Glasgow with 71 national teams participating. State visits were to Italy and the Vatican City in April and to France in June.

Reconciliation was the theme of this Christmas Broadcast:

In the ruins of the old Coventry Cathedral is a sculpture of a man and a woman reaching out to embrace each other ... inspired by the story of a woman who crossed Europe on foot after the war to find her husband.

In 1914, many people thought the war would be over by Christmas, but sadly by then the trenches were dug and the future shape of the war in Europe was set.

But, as we know, something remarkable did happen that Christmas, exactly a hundred years ago today.

Without any instruction or command, the shooting stopped and German and British soldiers met in No Man's Land. Photographs were taken and gifts exchanged. It was a Christmas truce. ...

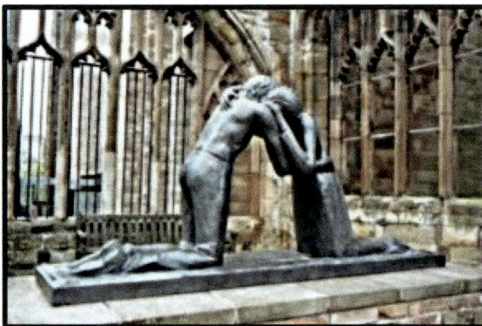

'Reconciliation' by Josefina de Vasconcellos at Coventry Cathedral

Christmas stamps 2014

For me, the life of Jesus Christ, the Prince of Peace, whose birth we celebrate today, is an inspiration and an anchor in my life.

A role model of reconciliation and forgiveness, he stretched out his hands in love, acceptance and healing. Christ's example has taught me to seek to respect and value all people, of whatever faith or none.

Sometimes it seems that reconciliation stands little chance in the face of war and discord. But, as the Christmas truce a century ago reminds us, peace and goodwill have lasting power in the hearts of men and women.

On that chilly Christmas Eve in 1914 many of the German forces sang Silent Night, its haunting melody inching across the line.

That carol is still much-loved today, a legacy of the Christmas truce, and a reminder to us all that even in the unlikeliest of places hope can still be found.

2015

Her Majesty Queen Elizabeth II became the longest-reigning British monarch on 9 September, 2015 (marked by Australia Post with the commemorative stamp, opposite). In a year marred with terrorist attacks and refugee crises she encouraged us to find hope amid the darkness.

There was a state visit to Germany in June and The Queen met with Commonwealth leaders in Malta in November. This message was recorded in Buckingham Palace's 18th Century Room.

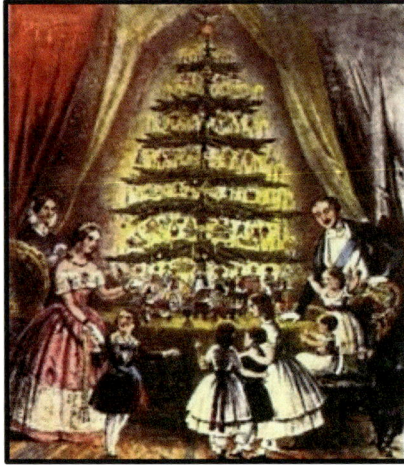

At this time of year, few sights evoke more feelings of cheer and goodwill than the twinkling lights of a Christmas tree.
The popularity of a tree at Christmas is due in part to my great-great grandparents, Queen Victoria and Prince Albert.
After this touching picture was published, many families wanted a Christmas tree of their own, and the custom soon spread. ...

Christmas stamps 2015

It is true that the world has had to confront moments of darkness this year, but the Gospel of John contains a verse of great hope, often read at Christmas carol services: "The light shines in the darkness, and the darkness has not overcome it".

One cause for thankfulness this summer was marking 70 years since the end of the Second World War. ...

At the end of that war, the people of Oslo began sending an annual gift of a Christmas tree for Trafalgar Square.

It has 500 light bulbs and is enjoyed not just by Christians but by people of all faiths, and of none. At the very top sits a bright star, to represent the Star of Bethlehem.

The custom of topping a tree also goes back to Prince Albert's time. For his family's tree, he chose an angel, helping to remind us that the focus of the Christmas story is on one particular family.

For Joseph and Mary, the circumstances of Jesus's birth - in a stable - were far from ideal, but worse was to come as the family was forced to flee the country.

It's no surprise that such a human story still captures our imagination and continues to inspire all of us who are Christians, the world over.

Despite being displaced and persecuted throughout his short life, Christ's unchanging message was not one of revenge or violence but simply that we should love one another.

Although it is not an easy message to follow, we shouldn't be discouraged; rather, it inspires us to try harder: to be thankful for the people who bring love and happiness into our own lives, and to look for ways of spreading that love to others, whenever and wherever we can.

2016

This year The Queen turned 90 on 21 April, 2016. To mark her 90th birthday, volunteers and supporters of the 600 charities of which she has been patron celebrated with lunch in the Mall. She talked about being inspired by the work they do.

The Christmas message was broadcast on **Facebook** for the first time **and on YouTube as well as on television and radio**.

The Queen praised the achievements of Olympian and Paralympian athletes at the **Rio Olympic Games** and reflected on the 60th anniversary of The Duke **of Edinburgh Awards** and the 40th anniversary of **The Prince's Trust.**

She spoke of the inspiration provided by ordinary people who are doing extraordinary things: the volunteers, carers, community organisers and good neighbours, *"unsung heroes whose quiet dedication makes them special."*

Opening the new Cambridge base of the East Anglian Air Ambulance, where Prince William worked as a helicopter pilot, moved her with the dedication of the highly skilled doctors, paramedics and crew.

The Queen quoted the words of Mother Teresa, now Saint Teresa of Calcutta: *"Not all of us can do great things. But we can do small things with great love."*

Christmas stamps 2016

United Kingdom commemorative stamps

At Christmas our attention is drawn to the birth of a baby some two thousand years ago. It was the humblest of beginnings, and his parents, Joseph and Mary, did not think they were important.

Jesus Christ lived obscurely for most of his life, and never travelled far. He was maligned and rejected by many, though he had done no wrong. And yet, billions of people now follow his teaching and find in him the guiding light for their lives. I am one of them because Christ's example helps me see the value of doing small things with great love, whoever does them and whatever they themselves believe.

The message of Christmas reminds us that inspiration is a gift to be given as well as received, and that love begins small but always grows.

I wish you all a very happy Christmas.

2017

This Christmas Broadcast, now seen on laptops, tablets and mobile phones, as well as broadcast on television and radio, began with the National Anthem by The Commonwealth Youth Orchestra and Choir and concluded with their beautiful rendition of the first and last verses of Midnight Clear:

It came upon the midnight clear,
That glorious song of old,
From angels bending near the earth,
To touch their harps of gold:
"Peace on the earth, goodwill to men,
From heaven's all-gracious King."
The world in solemn stillness lay,
To hear the angels sing.

For lo! the days are hastening on,
By prophet bards foretold,
When with the ever-circling years
Comes round the age of gold
When peace shall over all the earth
Its ancient splendours fling,
And the whole world give back the song
Which now the angels sing.

The broadcast included footage of the young Queen Elizabeth II speaking in her first television broadcast of 1957, 60 years previously. Other footage included Her Majesty visiting victims of the Manchester attack and she expressed her concern and sympathy for the victims and families affected by bombings in London and Manchester and by the Grenfell Tower fire. She also referred to **the Prince of Wales visiting the Caribbean in the aftermath of destructive hurricanes destroying whole communities there.**

The Queen mentioned her 70 years of marriage to Prince Philip who retired from solo public duties this year at 95 *"having, as he economically put it, done his bit."* Her Majesty noted that *"his support and unique sense of humour will remain as strong as ever."*

This broadcast referred to *"our homes as places of warmth, familiarity and love - of shared stories and memories - which is perhaps why, at this time of year, so many return to where they grew up. There is a timeless simplicity to the pull of home. ... We expect our homes to be a place of safety - sanctuary, even -"*

Christmas stamps 2017

Today, we celebrate Christmas, which, itself, is sometimes described as a festival of the home. Families travel long distances to be together.

Volunteers and charities, as well as many churches, arrange meals for the homeless and those who would otherwise be alone on Christmas Day. We remember the birth of Jesus Christ, whose only sanctuary was a stable in Bethlehem. He knew rejection, hardship and persecution.

And, yet, it is Jesus Christ's generous love and example which has inspired me through good times and bad. Whatever your own experience is this year, wherever and however you are watching, I wish you a peaceful and very happy Christmas.

2017 commemorated the 60th Anniversary of The Queen's first television broadcast in 1957, the 50th Anniversary of her first colour television broadcast in 1967, and 65 years of annual Christmas Messages from 1952.

During the years of her reign, the longest reigning British monarch, The Queen has provided stability, continuity, and innovation, and has appeared on television in our living rooms on Christmas afternoon throughout her reign.

The Queen made more than 260 official overseas visits to more than 100 different countries, and is committed to fostering harmony and progress among the Commonwealth nations.

Her annual official duties include attending the Commonwealth Day service and speech on the second Monday in March, Trooping the Colour on her official birthday in June at the Horse Guards Parade, laying a wreath at the Cenotaph every November, and she has not missed Royal Ascot since 1945.

The Royal Family usually stays at Balmoral in Scotland in August, Sandringham Estate for Christmas, Windsor Castle for Easter, and Buckingham Palace remains the headquarters of 'The Firm'.

The Queen invites a church minister to dinner each Sunday during her break at Balmoral. Famously, a Scottish minister once said grace there with the words, "For the delicious meal we are about to receive, and for the intercourse afterwards, may the Lord make us truly thankful."

Millions have reflected afterwards on the significance of Christmas following The Queen's Christmas Messages.

Appendix

Poets and songsters give us hymns and carols that help us celebrate Christmas.

Many YouTube recordings of The Queen's Christmas Broadcasts include choirs and bands singing and playing Christmas Carols. A list of these is included in the next pages of this Appendix.

This Appendix includes some well-known Christmas Carols that tell the Christmas Message and are found in the hymn books of most denominations. They are popular in Christmas celebrations and concerts such as Carols by Candlelight, and in churches in December.

Also included in the Appendix are some key resources related to The Queen's Christmas Broadcasts and some further information about *Renewal Journal* resources.

♕

Carols and Songs included in
The Queen's Christmas Broadcasts

1984
The First Noel by background orchestral music

1986
Away in a Manger by carollers in the royal stable

1998
Ding Dong Merrily on High by background singers

1999
Once in Royal David's City by St George's Chapel Boys Choir

2001
O Come all ye Faithful and **Hark the Herald Angels Sing** by choristers and a cathedral congregation

2004
Surrounded by His Love by Sir John Cass's Foundation Primary School Choir

2005
Hark the Herald Angels Sing by Her Majesty's Chapel Royal Boys Choir

2006
Ding Dong Merrily on High by youth choir

2007
O Little Town of Bethlehem by children singing in the background

2010
While Shepherds Watched by Her Majesty's Chapel Royal Boys Choir with children reading from Luke, chapter 2.

2011
O Little Town of Bethlehem by the Royal Guards Band

2012
In the Bleak Midwinter by the Military Wives Choir

2013
The First Noel by the Royal Guards Band

2014
Silent Night by the Royal Band

2015
Away in a Manger by the Children of Her Majesty's Chapel Royal

2016
Gloucestershire Wassail by the Royal Guards Band

2017
It Came upon the Midnight Clear by the Commonwealth Youth Orchestra and Choir

Find these recitals by searching 'YouTube The Queen's Christmas Message' with the year, eg. YouTube The Queen's Christmas Message 2017.

The following pages of this Appendix include many of the well-known carols, songs and hymns used at Christmas celebrations and in church services. They celebrate the Christmas Message with beautiful lyrics set to inspiring music.

O Come, All Ye Faithful

Adeste fideles læti triumphantes, | O come, all ye faithful, joyful and triumphant!
Venite, venite in Bethlehem. | O come ye, O come ye to Bethlehem;
Natum videte | Come and behold him
Regem angelorum: | Born the King of Angels:
Venite adoremus (3×) | O come, let us adore Him, (3×)
Dominum. | Christ the Lord.

Deum de Deo, lumen de lumine | God of God, light of light,
Gestant puellæ viscera | Lo, he abhors not the Virgin's womb;
Deum verum, genitum non factum. | Very God, begotten, not created:
Venite adoremus (3×) | O come, let us adore Him, (3×)
Dominum. | Christ the Lord.

Cantet nunc io, chorus angelorum; | Sing, choirs of angels, sing in exultation,
Cantet nunc aula cælestium, | Sing, all ye citizens of Heaven above!
Gloria, gloria in excelsis Deo, | Glory to God, glory in the highest:
Venite adoremus (3×) | O come, let us adore Him, (3×)
Dominum. | Christ the Lord.

Ergo qui natus die hodierna. | Yea, Lord, we greet thee, born this happy morning;
Jesu, tibi sit gloria, | Jesus, to thee be glory given!
Patris æterni Verbum caro factum. | Word of the Father, now in flesh appearing!
Venite adoremus (3×) | O come, let us adore Him, (3×)
Dominum. | Christ the Lord

Latin: John Francis Wade, 1751
English: Frederick Oakeley, 1841
Music: Adeste Fideles, 1751

Silent Night

Stille Nacht, heilige Nacht,
Alles schläft; einsam wacht
Nur das traute hochheilige Paar.
Holder Knabe im lockigen Haar,
Schlaf in himmlischer Ruh!
Schlaf in himmlischer Ruh!

Silent night, holy night,
All is calm, all is bright
Round yon virgin mother and child.
Holy infant, so tender and mild,
Sleep in heavenly peace,
Sleep in heavenly peace.

Stille Nacht, heilige Nacht,
Hirten erst kundgemacht
Durch der Engel Halleluja,
Tönt es laut von fern und nah:
Christ, der Retter ist da!
Christ, der Retter ist da!

Silent night, holy night,
Shepherds quake at the sight;
Glories stream from heaven afar,
Heavenly hosts sing Alleluia!
Christ the Saviour is born,
Christ the Saviour is born!

Stille Nacht, heilige Nacht,
Gottes Sohn, o wie lacht
Lieb' aus deinem göttlichen Mund,
Da uns schlägt die rettende Stund'.
Christ, in deiner Geburt!
Christ, in deiner Geburt!

Silent night, holy night,
Son of God, love's pure light;
Radiant beams from thy holy face
With the dawn of redeeming grace,
Jesus, Lord, at thy birth,
Jesus, Lord, at thy birth.

German: Joseph Mohr, 1818
English: John Freeman Young, 1859
Music: Franz Xaver Gruber, 1818

Angels from the Realms of Glory

Angels from the realms of Glory
Wing your flight o'er all the earth;
Ye who sang creation's story,
Now proclaim Messiah's birth:

Chorus:
Come and worship, come and worship,
Worship Christ, the newborn King.

Shepherds, in the fields abiding,
Watching o'er your flocks by night,
God with man is now residing,
Yonder shines the infant light:

Sages, leave your contemplations,
Brighter visions beam afar;
Seek the great Desire of nations,
Ye have seen his natal star:

Sinners, wrung with true repentance,
Doomed for guilt to endless pains,
Justice now revokes the sentence,
Mercy calls you—break your chains:

Though an infant now we view him,
He shall fill his Father's throne,
Gather all the nations to him;
Every knee shall then bow down:

All creation, join in praising
God the Father, Spirit, Son,
Evermore your voices raising,
To th'eternal Three in One:

Come and worship, come and worship
Worship Christ, the newborn King.

Lyrics: James Montgomery, 1816
Music: "Regent Square," Henry Smart, 1816

Angels We Have Heard on High

Angels we have heard on high
Sweetly singing o'er the plain
And the mountains in reply
Echoing their joyous strains

Chorus:
Gloria, in excelsis Deo!
Gloria, in excelsis Deo!

Shepherds, why this jubilee?
Why your joyous strains prolong?
What the gladsome tidings be?
Which inspire your heavenly songs?

Come to Bethlehem and see
Christ Whose birth the angels sing;
Come, adore on bended knee,
Christ, the Lord, the newborn King.

See Him in a manger laid,
Jesus, Lord of heaven and earth;
Mary, Joseph, lend your aid,
With us sing our Savior's birth.

Gloria, in excelsis Deo!
Gloria, in excelsis Deo!

Lyrics: James Chadwick, 1862
Music: French Carol
Music: "Gloria", Edward Shippen Barnes, 1937

Away in a Manger

Away in a manger, no crib for a bed,
The little Lord Jesus laid down his sweet head.
The stars in the bright sky looked down where he lay,
The little Lord Jesus asleep on the hay.

The cattle are lowing, the baby awakes,
But little Lord Jesus, no crying he makes.
I love thee, Lord Jesus! look down from the sky,
And stay by my cradle till morning is nigh.

Be near me, Lord Jesus; I ask thee to stay
Close by me forever, and love me I pray.
Bless all the dear children in thy tender care,
And take us to heaven to live with thee there.

Lyrics: Author unknown, 1885.
Music: William J. Kirkpatrick, 1895

Christians, Awake

Christians, awake! Salute the happy morn
whereon the Saviour of the world was born;
rise to adore the mystery of love,
which hosts of angels chanted from above;
with them the joyful tidings first begun,
of God incarnate and the virgin's Son.

Then to the watchful shepherds it was told,
who heard th'angelic herald's voice, "Behold,
I bring good tidings of a Saviour's birth
to you and all the nations of the earth;
this day hath God fulfilled His promised Word;
this day is born a Saviour, Christ the Lord."

This may we hope, th'angelic hosts among,
to sing, redeemed a glad triumphal song.
He that was born upon this joyful day
around us all His glory shall display.
Saved by His love, incessantly we sing
eternal praise to heav'n's almighty King.

Lyrics: John Byrom, 1741
Music: "Yorkshire," John Wainwright, 1750

Ding dong Merrily on High

Ding dong merrily on high,
In heav'n the bells are ringing:
Ding dong! Verily the sky
Is riv'n with angel singing.
Gloria, Hosanna in excelsis!

E'en so here below, below,
Let steeple bells be swungen,
And "Io, io, io!"
By priest and people sungen.

Pray you, dutifully prime
Your matin chime, ye ringers
May you beautifully rime
Your evetime song, ye singers
Gloria, Hosanna in excelsis!
[Glory. Hosanna in the highest!]

Lyrics: George Ratcliffe Woodward, 1924
Music: **Branle** de l'Official, 1589

Joy to the World

Joy to the world, the Lord is come!
Let earth receive her King;
Let every heart prepare Him room,
And heav'n and nature sing,
And heav'n and nature sing,
And heav'n, and heav'n, and nature sing.

Joy to the earth, the Savior reigns!
Let men their songs employ;
While fields and floods, rocks, hills, and plains
Repeat the sounding joy,
Repeat the sounding joy,
Repeat, repeat, the sounding joy.

No more let sins and sorrows grow,
Nor thorns infest the ground;
He comes to make His blessings flow
Far as the curse is found,
Far as the curse is found,
Far as, far as, the curse is found.

He rules the world with truth and grace,
And makes the nations prove
The glories of His righteousness,
And wonders of His love,
And wonders of His love,
And wonders, wonders, of His love.

Lyrics: Isaac Watts, 1719
Music: Arranged from George Friedrich Handel, 1833

In the Bleak Mid-Winter

In the bleak mid-winter
Frosty wind made moan;
Earth stood hard as iron,
Water like a stone;
Snow had fallen, snow on snow,
Snow on snow,
In the bleak mid-winter
Long ago.

Our God, heaven cannot hold Him
Nor earth sustain,
Heaven and earth shall flee away
When He comes to reign:
In the bleak mid-winter
A stable-place sufficed
The Lord God Almighty —
Jesus Christ.

Enough for Him, whom Cherubim
Worship night and day,
A breastful of milk
And a mangerful of hay;
Enough for Him, whom Angels
Fall down before,
The ox and ass and camel
Which adore.

Angels and Archangels
May have gathered there,
Cherubim and seraphim
Thronged the air;
But only His Mother
In her maiden bliss
Worshipped the Beloved
With a kiss.

What can I give Him,
Poor as I am? —
If I were a Shepherd
I would bring a lamb;
If I were a Wise Man
I would do my part, —
Yet what I can I give Him, —
Give my heart.

Lyrics: Christina Rossetti, 1872
Music: "Cranham," Gustav Holst, 1906

It Came upon the Midnight Clear

It came upon the midnight clear,
That glorious song of old,
From angels bending near the earth,
To touch their harps of gold:
"Peace on the earth, goodwill to men,
From heaven's all-gracious King."
The world in solemn stillness lay,
To hear the angels sing.

Still through the cloven skies they come,
With peaceful wings unfurled,
And still their heavenly music floats
O'er all the weary world;
Above its sad and lowly plains,
They bend on hovering wing,
And ever o'er its babel sounds
The blessed angels sing.

Yet with the woes of sin and strife
The world has suffered long;
Beneath the angel-strain have rolled
Two thousand years of wrong;
And man, at war with man, hears not
The love-song which they bring;
O hush the noise, ye men of strife,
And hear the angels sing.

And ye, beneath life's crushing load,
Whose forms are bending low,
Who toil along the climbing way
With painful steps and slow,
Look now! for glad and golden hours
Come swiftly on the wing.
O rest beside the weary road,
And hear the angels sing!

For lo! the days are hastening on,
By prophet bards foretold,
When with the ever-circling years
Comes round the age of gold
When peace shall over all the earth
Its ancient splendours fling,
And the whole world give back the song
Which now the angels sing.

Lyrics: Edmund H. Sears, 1849
Music: "Carol," Richard Storrs Willis, 1850
Music: "Noel," English Melody adapted by Arthur Sullivan, 1874

O Little Town of Bethlehem

O little town of Bethlehem
 How still we see thee lie!
Above thy deep and dreamless sleep
    The silent stars go by.
Yet in thy dark streets shineth
    The everlasting Light;
The hopes and fears of all the years
    Are met in thee to-night.

O morning stars, together
    Proclaim the holy birth!
And praises sing to God the King,
    And peace to men on earth.
For Christ is born of Mary
    And gathered all above,
While mortals sleep the Angels keep
    Their watch of wondering love.

How silently, how silently,
    The wondrous gift is given;
So God imparts to human hearts
    The blessings of His Heaven.
No ear may hear His coming,
    But in this world of sin,
Where meek souls will receive Him still,
    The dear Christ enters in.

O holy Child of Bethlehem,
    Descend to us, we pray!
Cast out our sin and enter in,
    Be born in us to-day.
We hear the Christmas angels,
    The great glad tidings tell;
O come to us, abide with us,
    Our Lord Emmanuel!

Lyrics: Phillips Brooks, 1868
Music: "St. Louis," Lewis Henry Redner, 1868

Once in Royal David's City

Once in royal David's city
Stood a lowly cattle shed,
Where a mother laid her Baby
In a manger for His bed:
Mary was that mother mild,
Jesus Christ her little Child.

He came down to earth from heaven,
Who is God and Lord of all,
And His shelter was a stable,
And His cradle was a stall;
With the poor, and mean, and lowly,
Lived on earth our Saviour holy.

And through all His wondrous childhood
He would honour and obey,
Love and watch the lowly maiden,
In whose gentle arms He lay:
Christian children all must be
Mild, obedient, good as He.

For he is our childhood's pattern;
Day by day, like us He grew;
He was little, weak and helpless,
Tears and smiles like us He knew;
And He feeleth for our sadness,
And He shareth in our gladness.

And our eyes at last shall see Him,
Through His own redeeming love;
For that Child so dear and gentle
Is our Lord in heaven above,
And He leads His children on
To the place where He is gone.

6. Not in that poor lowly stable,
With the oxen standing by,
We shall see Him; but in heaven,
Set at God's right hand on high;
Where like stars His children crowned
All in white shall wait around.

Lyrics: Cecil Frances Humphreys Alexander, 1848
Music: "Irby," Henry John Gauntlett, 1849

Surrounded by His Love

The Lord is my shepherd
He'll watch over me
Whatever I go through
He's all that I need
Wherever he leads me
I know sure enough
I will live my life
Surrounded by his love

The Lord is my shepherd
He'll stay by my side
When I feel afraid
In the darkest of nights
I'm safe in the hands
Of the Father above
I will live my life
Surrounded by his love

And I will sing his praise

Surely goodness and mercy are following me
All of the days of my life
Now and forever my home will be
Here in the house of the Lord
Surrounded by his love

The Lord is my shepherd
He's gentle and strong
I know in his presence
I'll always belong
The peace that he gives me
Is more than enough
I will live my life
Surrounded by his love

Lyrics: Paul Field, 1997
Music: Daybreak Music/Elevation, 1997

The First Noel

The First Noel the angel did say
Was to certain poor shepherds
in fields as they lay;
In fields as they lay, keeping their sheep,
On a cold winter's night that was so deep.

Chorus:
Noel, Noel, Noel, Noel,
Born is the King of Israel.

They looked up and saw a star
Shining in the east beyond them far,
And to the earth it gave great light,
And so it continued both day and night.

And by the light of that same star
Three wise men came from country far;
To seek for a king was their intent,
And to follow the star wherever it went.

This star drew nigh to the northwest,
O'er Bethlehem it took it rest,
And there it did both stop and stay
Right over the place where Jesus lay.

Then entered in those wise men three
Full reverently upon their knee,
and offered there in his presence
Their gold, and myrrh, and frankincense.

Then let us all with one accord
Sing praises to our heavenly Lord;
That hath made heaven and earth of naught,
And with his blood mankind hath bought.

Noel, Noel, Noel, Noel,
Born is the King of Israel.

Lyrics: William Sandys, Davies Gilbert, 1823
Music: John Stainer, 1871

While Shepherds Watched their Flocks

While shepherds watched their flocks by night,
All seated on the ground,
The angel of the Lord came down,
And glory shone around.

"Fear not!" said he, for mighty dread
Had seized their troubled mind;
"Glad tidings of great joy I bring
To you and all mankind.

"To you, in David's town, this day
Is born of David's line
A Saviour, who is Christ the Lord,
And this shall be the sign:

"The heav'nly Babe you there shall find
To human view displayed,
All meanly wrapped in swathing bands,
And in a manger laid."

Thus spake the seraph and forthwith
Appeared a shining throng
Of angels praising God on high,
Who thus addressed their song:

"All glory be to God on high,
And to the Earth be peace;
Good will henceforth from heav'n to men
Begin and never cease!"

Lyrics: Nathan Tate, 1700
Music: George Friedrich Handel, 1728

Messiah - Selections

Messiah is an English-language oratorio composed in 1741 by George Friedrich Handel, with a scriptural text compiled by Charles Jennens from the King James Bible, and from the version of the *Psalms* included with the *Book of Common Prayer*.

In Part I the text begins with prophecies by Isaiah and others, and moves to the annunciation to the shepherds, the only "scene" taken from the Gospels. **In Part II**, Handel concentrates on the Passion and ends with the "Hallelujah" chorus. **In Part III** he covers the resurrection of the dead and Christ's glorification in heaven. It is reported that when King George II attended a royal performance of *Messiah* he stood up for the *Hallelujah Chorus* in honour of the King of kings. When the king stood everyone in his presence had to stand. So it became tradition for the audience to stand up when the *Hallelujah Chorus* is sung, as millions of us have done in honour of the King of kings.

Chorus — Isaiah 9:6
For unto us a Child is born, unto us a Son is given: and the government shall be upon His shoulder: and His name shall be called Wonderful, Counsellor, the mighty God, the everlasting Father, the Prince of Peace.
Pifa (Pastoral Symphony)
Soprano Recitative — Luke 2:8-11, 13
There were shepherds abiding in the field, keeping watch over their flocks by night.
And lo! the angel of the Lord came upon them, and the glory of the Lord shone round about them: and they were sore afraid.
And the angel said unto them, Fear not; for, behold, I bring you good tidings of great joy, which shall be to all people. For unto you is born this day in the city of David a Saviour, which is Christ the Lord.
And suddenly there was with the angel a multitude of the heavenly host praising God, and saying,
Chorus — Luke 2:14
Glory to God in the highest, and peace on earth, good will toward men.

Chorus — Revelation 19:6, 11:15, 19:16
Hallelujah! for the Lord God Omnipotent reigneth.
The Kingdom of this world is become the Kingdom of our Lord, and of His Christ; and He shall reign for ever and ever.
King of kings, and Lord of lords.
Hallelujah!

Lyrics: Holy Bible, Authorised Version, 1611, arranged by Charles Jennens, 1741
Music: George Friedrich Handel, 1741

Resources

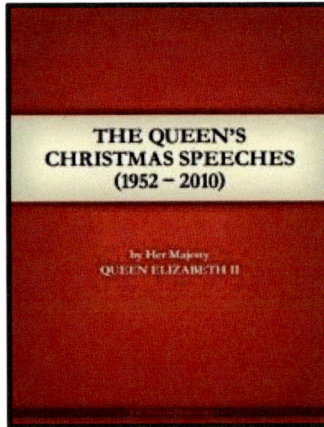

Her Majesty Queen Elizabeth II. *The Queen's Christmas Speeches (1952 - 2010)*. The British Monarchy. Kindle Edition.

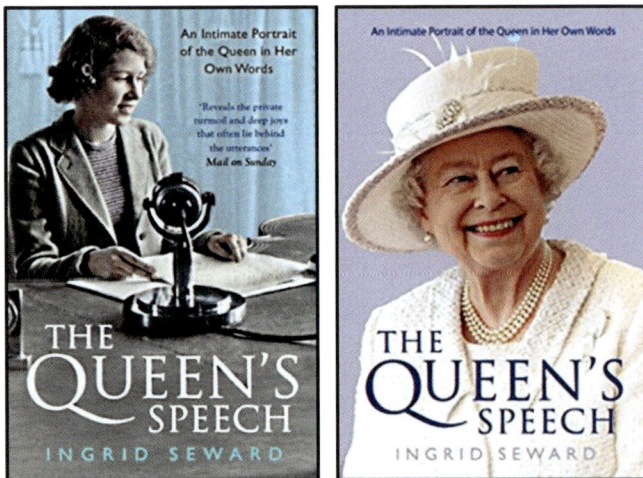

Ingrid Seward (2015), *The Queen's Speech*. Simon & Schuster.

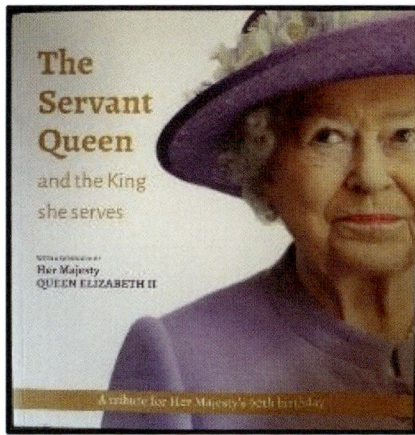

William Shawcross (2016). *The Servant Queen and the King She Serves.*
The Bible Society.

The Royal Family, *The Christmas Broadcast*
https://www.royal.uk/christmas-broadcast-1952 [annual broadcast scripts]

Wikipedia, *Royal Christmas Message.*
https://en.wikipedia.org/wiki/Royal_Christmas_Message

The Royal Family: Facebook
https://www.facebook.com/TheBritishMonarchy/

Cue The Queen: Celebrating the Christmas Message (BBC One, YouTube)

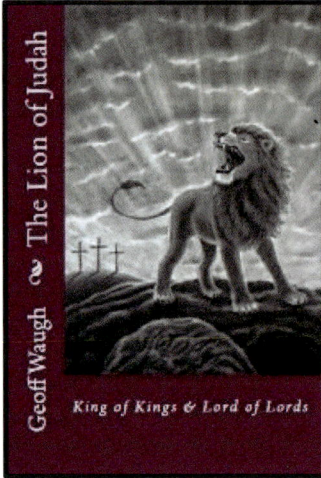

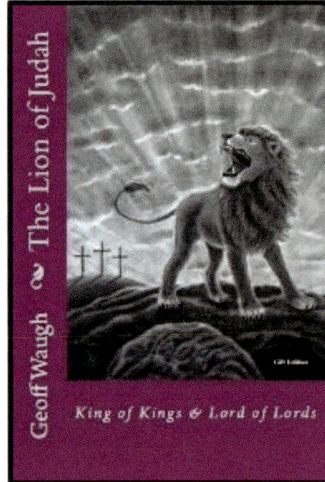

Basic Edition in print and Gift Edition in colour

The Lion of Judah: King of Kings and Lord of Lords
A devotional commentary on Jesus, the Lion of Judah
Six books compiled into one volume.

Introduction

1. The Titles of Jesus

2. The Reign of Jesus

3. The Life of Jesus

4. The Death of Jesus

5. The Resurrection of Jesus

6. The Spirit of Jesus

Conclusion: The Lion of Judah

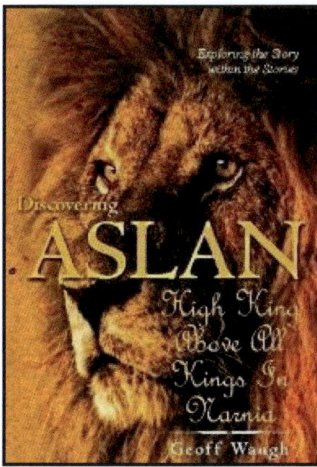

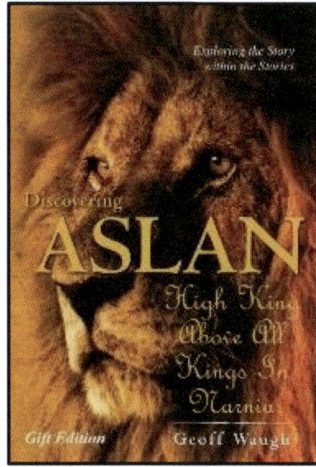

Basic Edition in print and Gift Edition in colour

Discovering Aslan: High King above all Kings in Narnia
A devotional commentary on Jesus, the Lion of Judah
Seven books compiled into one volume.

Prologue & Introduction

1. The Lion, the Witch and the Wardrobe
"Aslan is on the move"

2. Prince Caspian
"Every year you grow you will find me bigger"

3. The Voyage of the Dawn Treader
"By knowing me here for a little, you may know me better there"

4. The Silver Chair
"Aslan's instructions always work: there are no exceptions"

5. The Horse and His Boy
"High King above all kings in Narnia"

6. The Magician's Nephew
"I give you yourselves ... and I give you myself"

7. The Last Battle
"Further up and further in"

Conclusion & Epilogue

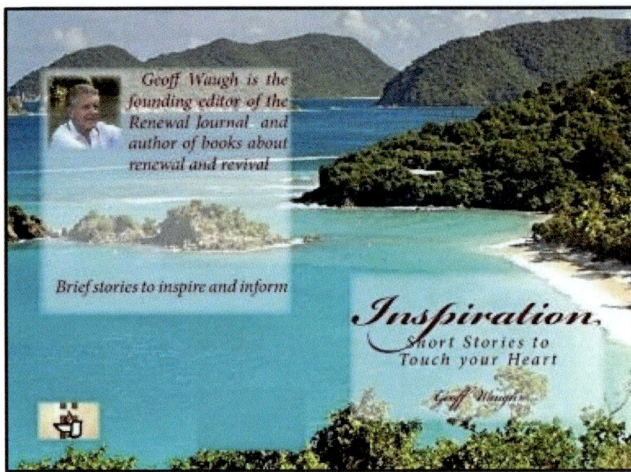

Basic Edition in print and Gift Edition in colour

Inspiration

Short stories to touch your heart

1 Saying Grace
2 The Surgeon
3 Cost of a Miracle_
4 The Son
5 What would you do?
6 You are my Sunshine
7 Special Olympics
8 Everything we do is Important_
9 Friends
10 Coming Home
11 Red Marbles_
12 Surprise Hidden in Plain Sight
13 Choices_
14 Prayer PUSH
15 Cracked-pots
16 A Girls' Prayer
17 A Boy's Insights
18 Shirley and Marcy
19 One Liners
20 I Choose
21 The Gold and Ivory Tablecloth
22 Behold the Man
23 Family Worship
24 Eternity

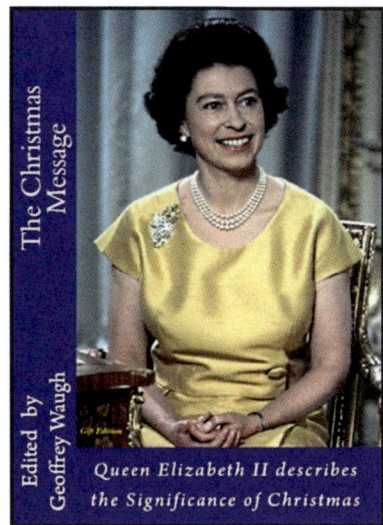

Basic Edition in print and Gift Edition in colour

The Christmas Message:
Queen Elizabeth II describes the Significance of Christmas

This book is also available with the original sub-title:

The Christmas Message:
Reflections on the Significance of Christmas
from The Queen's Christmas Broadcasts

All these books are updated annually after December 25.

Renewal Journal

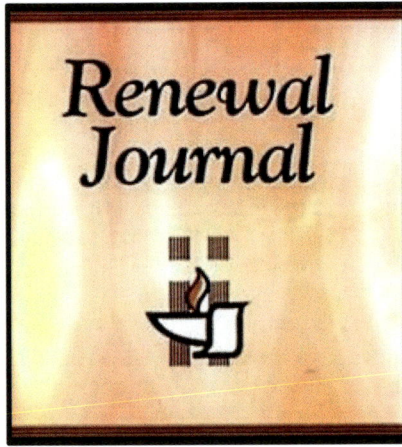

www.renewaljournal.com

The Renewal Journal website gives links to

Renewal Journals

Books

Blogs

Free subscription gives you updates for

new Blogs and free offers including

free eBooks

About the Editor

The Rev Dr Geoff Waugh is the founding editor of the *Renewal Journal* and author of books on ministry and mission. He taught Anglican, Catholic and Uniting Church (formerly Congregational, Methodist and Presbyterian) students in Trinity Theological College and the School of Theology of Griffith University as well as at Christian Heritage College in Brisbane, Australia. He taught in schools and Bible Colleges in Papua New Guinea and in the South Pacific with Baptist and Churches of Christ missions and led short term missions in Africa, Europe, South-East Asia and in the South Pacific islands.

His books and the *Renewal Journals* are available from Amazon, Kindle and Distributors.

Geoff and Meg have been blessed with three adult children and eight grandchildren, and have celebrated Christmas with five generations including parents and grandparents, proclaiming the Christmas Message:

"Fear not: for, behold, I bring you good tidings of great joy, which shall be to all people. For unto you is born this day in the city of David a Saviour, who is Christ the Lord."

Printed in Great Britain
by Amazon